Acclaim for *America's Competitive Secret*

"Judy B. Rosener chronicles the barriers to full use of women's talents—and the cost to business."—*Washington Post*

". . . a straightforward and readable guide that will help each side understand the other's attitude about women in management."—*St. Louis Post Dispatch*

"In her simple, no nonsense style, Rosener demystifies why and how men and women respond to gender in the workplace."—*Women in Management Review*

"American women [Rosener] argues, are an untapped, or at least an underutilized competitive resource."—*The New York Times*

"Rosener has written an arguement designed to persuade organizations and the mostly male executives who head them that their failure to make the most of the available talent pool is costing them money."—*Training*

"By exposing the issues and possibilities of women-as-managers in the first book ever written on the subject, Rosener addresses the topic head-on and shows us all how to come out winners."—*The Atlanta Small Business Monthly*

"Read the preface to *America's Competitive Secret* and you'll be hooked. [It] reveals Judy Rosener's energy, passion, personality and commitment to the fuller utilization of women in the workplace so compellingly that reading further is a must."—*Women's Enterprise*

Praise for Judy B. Rosener

"Judy Rosener has a theory. And if the professor . . . is correct, her supposition has import for every U.S. business."—*San Francisco Business Times*

"A look at Rosener's 17-page curriculum vitae reveals much about a woman who's always been ahead of her time . . . Certainly no one questions [her] ability to crack open windows, and sometimes even thick corporate ceilings."—*Los Angeles Times*

"Rosener . . . is in demand by Fortune 500 executives trying to find out why women are leaving larger companies at three to five times the rate of men."—*Harper's Bazaar*

America's
Competitive
Secret

America's Competitive Secret

Women Managers

Judy B. Rosener

1995

OXFORD UNIVERSITY PRESS
New York   Oxford

Oxford University Press

Oxford   New York
Athens   Auckland   Bangkok   Bogotá   Bombay
Buenos Aires   Calcutta   Cape Town   Dar es Salaam
Delhi   Florence   Hong Kong   Istanbul   Karachi
Kuala Lumpur   Madras   Madrid   Melbourne
Mexico City   Nairobi   Paris   Singapore
Taipei   Tokyo   Toronto   Warsaw

and associated companies in
Berlin   Ibadan

Library of Congress Cataloging-in-Publication Data
Rosener, Judy B.
America's competitive secret: utilizing women as
a management strategy   Judy B. Rosener.
p.   cm.
Includes bibliographical references and index.
ISBN 0-19-508079-3
ISBN 0-19-511914-2 (Pbk.)
1. Women executives—United States.
2. Feminism—United States.   I. Title.
HD6054.4.U6R67   1995   658.4'0082—dc20   95-11808

10 9 8 7 6 5 4
Printed in the United States of America

To Joe, my bright, patient, supportive, incredible husband of forty-three years, who is an intellectual and emotional anchor. He always makes me feel loved and valued.

To my late mother, Sylvia L. Bogen, a wonderful, dynamic, highly intelligent woman whose talents were underutilized because she was born at the wrong time.

To our terrific grown children, Lynn, Doug, and Janet, who with good humor and understanding have endured a mother preoccupied for three years with this book.

Preface

This book is intended for executives and managers who want to improve their organization's bottom line, and for women who wonder why their career paths so often seem to be shaped by the fact that they are female. It is also written for men who realize that women are in the workplace to stay and who want to understand the economic as well as social and psychological implications of having women as peers and competitors.

Much has been written about management strategy, human resources, and workplace issues associated with women. However, rarely have the three been studied together. I am convinced there is a common thread that runs through much of the research in these three areas, that of economic competitiveness. My purpose in writing this book has been to make that thread visible. I consider myself a synthesizer and translator. I have tried to avoid academic jargon and write in language that is easily understood and related to work practices and the bottom line.

Because there are always difficulties in translation, and because issues and data change rapidly, it is important to make some qualifications about the book's content. First, the data found in the tables and in the body of the book are as current as I could make them given the time lag between manuscript delivery and publication. Second, the two leadership styles discussed throughout the book, command-and-control and interactive, are "ideal types." That is, they represent two ends of a style continuum from authoritative to collaborative and are thus helpful in making comparisons. When I associate the command-and-control style with men and the interactive style with women, I do not mean *all* men or *all* women. Similarly, the generalizations in the book are just that—generalizations. They are not meant to be applied universally.

A number of the terms found throughout need clarification. I use the words "sex" and "gender" interchangeably even though I know some purists may find this troublesome. Sex has to do with biology, and gender has to do with norms of behavior, but they are so closely related that I have chosen not to distinguish between them. The term "glass ceiling" is a metaphor for the barriers to advancement that exist for women because they are women. I use the term "underutilization" as a broad umbrella under which glass ceilings occur—that is, one manifestation of underutilization is the glass ceiling. Finally, I use the term "reward system" to mean the way in which organizations confer rewards and value certain types of behavior. A reward system can be formal or informal, but in either case it shapes decisions.

In general, when I speak of "women," I mean those who have specialized training or education that is assumed to be preparatory for managerial or executive positions. They are women who anticipate having careers, not just jobs. It is difficult to define this group of women precisely, so I use the terms "professional" and "managerial" interchangeably, knowing that the two categories are not always identical.

It is important to note that most of my observations are based on the experiences of white women in an organizational environment dominated by white men. That is because the majority of professional women and men are white. In Chapters 5 and 6, I have included brief discussions of the experiences of black men and women, as reminders that issues tend to look very different at the intersection of race and gender. These discussions are in no way offered as in-depth treatments.

In this connection, I should stress that I believe *gen-*

der issues are a subset of cultural diversity issues. Although my main topic is gender, many of the concepts and ideas in this book are equally valid for people of color, gays and lesbians, and anybody who is different from those at the top of most American institutions. By focusing on women, it is not my intent to suggest that only women are underutilized. Blacks, Latinos, Asians, and other groups are also devalued and underutilized, as are some white males. However, in absolute numbers, women make up the single largest underutilized group, and therefore the single largest pool of untapped leadership potential. Furthermore, if women's issues aren't addressed, issues of race, ethnicity, and sexual orientation aren't likely to be addressed either.

America's Competitive Secret has many antecedents in my own experience. I graduated from UCLA in 1951 with a major in sociology. Why sociology? Because like most women in those days, I had no career plans. I didn't like math or science, and sociology seemed as good a major as any. Like other women, I went to college to broaden my horizons and find a husband. That's what most of us did. As it turns out, I found a wonderful husband, and my UCLA education prepared me well for my current interests. I was fortunate to have outstanding scholars (then young assistant professors) as teachers. Philip Selznick, Abraham Kaplan, Walter Goldschmidt, Ralph Turner, and Donald Cressey exposed me to ideas that gave me a foundation for understanding organizations and organizational change.

For fifteen years after graduating from UCLA, I was a Newport Beach housewife tending my garden, improving my tennis, and being a mother and community volunteer. In 1965 a new University of California campus opened its doors in Irvine, a city near where I lived. UCI's first dean of the School of Social Sciences was Jim March, a respected scholar of organizational behavior, now at Stanford. We had met socially, and he suggested I return to school. Today this would be unremarkable, but in those days middle-aged women rarely went back to school. Jim March was sending a message that he felt older women could be graduate students. In the context of this book, he understood that the talent represented by women was underutilized in academe.

Through a series of odd circumstances, in 1972 I ended up teaching a class in the small new UCI Graduate School of Management. At the time, I was equipped with a master's degree, no teaching experience, and no career aspirations. In 1976 Dean Lyman Porter told me I would have to get a Ph.D. if I wanted to continue teaching. The campus was now established, and only "real professors" would be retained. I was forty-seven years old, teaching two classes, and serving full-time on the California Coastal Commission, a state regulatory agency. Our three children were in college or college-bound, and they all said, "Go for it!" I did. I was almost fifty when I got my Ph.D. in 1979 and found myself with an academic career. I received a full-time permanent faculty position at the age of fifty-three. So much for how I unexpectedly became an academic.

It was my eldest daughter, Lynn, a graduate of Stanford doing futures research at the Stanford Research Institute in 1979, who introduced me to the issue of gender and leadership. She and a colleague at SRI, Peter Schwartz, were writing an article at the request of the National Organization for Women. In retrospect, I realize that their article—"Women, Leadership, and the 1980s: What Kind of Leaders Do We Need?"—posed a key question that this book attempts to address. As a result of the article, Lynn was asked to write about gender and leadership for an academic journal. Not familiar with academic writing, she suggested we work together. The result of our collaboration, "Alpha + Beta = A New Effectiveness: Leaders and Followers in the 1990s," was published in 1986 as a chapter in *Leaders and Followers: Challenge for the Future,* edited by Jon Von Til and Louis Zurcher.

In "Alpha + Beta" Lynn and I talked about the importance of perception and suggested that men and women perceive issues and make decisions differently. For that reason, we felt that male and female leaders would probably have different impacts on organizations. We had no hard evidence; our ideas were based on conjecture. We also said there was no one best leadership style, but that the female, or beta, style (called "interactive" in this book) offered advantages not found in the male, or alpha, style ("command-and-control"). We noted that the two leadership styles were not mutually exclusive, that most effective leaders used both, but that men tended to prefer the alpha style and women the beta style. We concluded that if organizations valued and rewarded the beta leadership style in the same way they valued and rewarded the alpha style, there would be a new kind of organizational effectiveness.

That concept of a new effectiveness is implicit in the concept of enlightened management strategy advocated in *America's Competitive Secret.* I will consider the book a success if it inspires leaders to appreciate the connection between organizational effectiveness and the full utilization of professional women.

Irvine, Calif.   J.B.R.
March 1995

the feminization
of america?

Acknowledgments

This book has been a collaborative effort. Laura Brown and Herb Addison of Oxford University Press deserve much of the credit for its existence. Without Laura's belief in its message and her ongoing support and guidance, the book would have not been written. Herb's many constructive suggestions and his encouragement as my editor were particularly helpful.

Kim Jaussi also deserves a great deal of credit. I discovered her in the fall of 1990 in a small coffee shop she owned with another young woman. I was one of a motley group of walkers, joggers, and newspaper readers who met at the Coffee Pub early in the morning to reward ourselves with muffins and cappuccino. It was an intimate place, and the conversation often turned to work. Kim, a 1990 Smith College graduate, was interested when I told her I was writing a book about women and economic competitiveness. She offered to help me, saying she missed the intellectual challenge associated with being on a college campus, and I accepted her offer. Kim became my primary research assistant. At first I asked her to track down citations and do the routine tasks research assistants do. More recently she has provided substantive insights and suggestions about the book's content. I can't overemphasize her contribution, or the value of her sense of humor and patience as I struggled to articulate my ideas. She is precisely the kind of woman whose talents represent the valuable economic resource I discuss throughout this book.

Many others have made contributions to the book by virtue of their friendship and expertise. Foremost among them are Lee Gardenswartz and Anita Rowe, general management and diversity consultants, professional colleagues, authors, and close friends. They shared their knowledge with me, provided emotional support, and always showed an interest in my work. I am also indebted to Marilyn Loden, my co-author on *Workforce America! Managing Employee Diversity as a Vital Resource,* and author of *Feminine Leadership, or How to Succeed in Business without Being One of the Boys,* a 1985 book that helped me clarify my ideas about gender and leadership. And to Joy Johannessen at Oxford University Press, a special thank-you for helping me navigate some turbulent conceptual and grammatical waters.

Beatrice Young, president of Bea Young Associates in Glencoe, Illinois, is another colleague, friend, and management consultant who acted as a sounding board. She is responsible for many of the ideas in Chapters 8 and 9. Nancy Woodhull, one of the founding editors of *USA Today,* and an expert on women and communication issues, was generous with her help, as were Joline Godfrey, author of *Our Wildest Dreams,* and academics Rita Mae Kelly, Lyn Kathlene, Nancy Adler, and Sue Thomas, who provided me with many references and insights. My cousin Dr. Joe E. Bogen, scholar and neurosurgeon, introduced me to the sex/brain literature and explained it well. I also want to thank Joe Flowers, journalist, innovative thinker, and director of the Change Project in Sausalito, California, for his wisdom on the subject of how men feel about the emergence of women professionals. Frank Quevedo, director of affirmative action for Southern California Edison, and George Dean, founder of 50/50 by the Year 2000, an organization that promotes gender equality in federal and state government, have been a terrific volunteer clipping service for articles relevant to my interests.

Former M.B.A. students Sarah Lee and Mitsuyo Arimoto helped me obtain information on Asian women. Professor Beverly Alimo-Metcalfe of the Nuffield Institute for Health at the University of Leeds, an expert on women and work, and particularly on performance assessment, has been a wonderful resource. Through the marvel of international fax, she provided me with a wealth of data about women in the United Kingdom.

Caroline Langridge, director of the Women's Unit in the National Health Service, and Ann James, formerly a research fellow at Kings Fund College, were responsible for my traveling to the United Kingdom to study changes taking place in the National Health Service. It was Caroline Langridge's idea for me to attend a conference of the European Community (now the European Union) in Birmingham, England, where I learned about the important directives concerning women described in Chapter 10. Valerie Hammond, chief executive of Roffey Park Management Institute, U.K., a longtime colleague and one of the most knowledgeable authorities on European women in management, helped me conduct a survey of women in European Union countries. She also kept me abreast of developments abroad, particularly in England.

I want to thank all those, too many to mention, who granted me interviews or talked to me in offices, at cocktail parties, and at corporate retreats. Some asked to remain anonymous; in those cases, I have changed names and sometimes characteristics of organizations so they could not be identified. However, all the stories in the book are based on true accounts. Their names are scattered among its pages. I particularly want to thank Raydean Acevedo, Mary Midyette, Judith Rogala, and Linda Cyrog-Giacomi.

I cannot tell a lie. I came across many of my sources in the first-class cabins of airplanes as I flew around the world on my way to speaking engagements and professional meetings. I saved every business card I was given, and many of the people who handed me those cards received phone calls asking for clarification of conversations and permission to use their comments in the book.

Much of the book was written while I was teaching at the Graduate School of Management at the University of California, Irvine (UCI), where Dean Dennis Aigner made few demands on my time, knowing of my preoccupation with the manuscript. Two colleagues, Richard Brahm and Richard McKenzie, deserve special thanks. Richard Brahm introduced me to the literature on management strategy, and Richard McKenzie kept reminding me of the importance of economics. As we shared coffee, they heard more about this book than they probably care to recall. I'm also indebted to Valeska Wolf and Melinda Johnson. Valeska typed so many rewrites of each chapter and reformatted so many footnotes she must think about them in her sleep. Melinda, my UCI secretary/assistant at the time, kept me smiling, took care of all the details in my life, and was always there when I needed her.

Numerous companies, government agencies, and non-profits provided me with a wealth of information through conversations with their executives and employees. These organizations include Xerox, American President Companies, Boise Cascade, Gibson, Dunn and Crutcher, Petit Martin, CSX, TRW, Hammond Company, McDonnell Douglas, Hughes, Southern California Edison, Norfolk Southern, Anderson Consultants, Texas Instruments, Beckman Instruments, Price Waterhouse, United California Savings Bank, Motorola, Bank of America, Wells Fargo Bank, AT&T, Lathrop/Watkins, Nestlé, IBM, the IRS, the U.S. Forestry Service, the Junior League, Leadership California and Leadership America, Baxter International, and Premier Hospitals.

I want to thank my agents at the Leigh Bureau, Tom Neilssen, Les Tuerk, Robin Wolfson, Danny Stern, and Fran Weber, who introduced me to many organizations where I talked with executives interested in cultural diversity and gender issues as they relate to management strategy.

Finally, I want to thank Professor Rosabeth Kanter, former editor of the *Harvard Business Review*, who published my article "Ways Women Lead" in 1990, and Adrienne Hall, who gave her my name. In her capacity as associate editor at the *Harvard Business Review*, Geri Willigan masterfully guided my hand, and her contribution to "Ways Women Lead" was considerable. I will always be indebted to these three women, for it was this article that captured the attention of Oxford University Press.

Contents

America's Competitive Secret

1

The Bottom Line

This book proposes an audacious idea: that leveraging the talents of professional women will lead to more innovative, productive, and profitable organizations. Implicit in this idea is another: that any country whose businesses fully utilize their professional women—which means including them in top management—will ultimately be more competitive at home and abroad. I hope to convince readers that the special abilities women have by virtue of being women should be highly regarded because they constitute an underutilized economic resource. I also hope to convince them that while gender equality in the workplace has been seen in the past as an issue of social justice, today it is an economic imperative.

The Way We Were

Until recently, the United States was king of the hill. Our military might was awesome and kept enemies at bay. Our technological prowess and highly skilled labor force were the envy of all. A "Made in America" label brought high prices around the world. But something happened on the way to the 1990s. America experienced a civil rights movement, a women's movement, a sexual revolution, a technological revolution, and a decade of inflation. Women joined the professional ranks seeking economic survival as well as self-fulfillment. Concerns about pay equity, sexual discrimination, and parental leave began to surface in even the most conventional organizations, and women began in earnest to share their workplace experiences with each other. At the same time, the United States began to lose economic ground in sectors such as steel, shipbuilding, consumer electronics, small cars, and machine tools. Gradually, the changing economic climate forced corporate leaders to question the way their organizations were run, and academics to examine traditional theories of management.

Management practices in American organizations have generally followed the command-and-control leadership model, which stresses clear lines of authority, the accumulation of power and information, a win-lose decision process, and the value of sameness and homogeneity. But the past several decades have shown that Harlan Cleveland was right when he predicted in 1972 that in the future "the organizations that get things done will no longer be hierarchical pyramids with most of the real control at the top. They will be systems—interlaced webs of tension in which control is loose, power is diffused, and centers of decision are plural."[1]

In the 1980s the shock of seeing markets disappear and the value of the dollar plummet intensified interest in new organizational structures and alternatives to the theory of scientific management that dominated management philosophy at the time. In a much-discussed 1987 article, "Making Management Decisions: The Role of Intuition and Emotion," Herbert Simon made the case that managerial decision making is not entirely scientific and that intuition plays a productive if often unrecognized role.[2] Peter Senge's

1990 bestseller, *The Fifth Discipline,* also challenged the notion of scientific management and proposed a holistic theory of systems thinking.[3] Senge's ideas captured the fancy of American executives and stimulated renewed interest in the learning organization, a concept pioneered by John Gardner and others decades earlier.[4]

Peter Drucker also took a slap at conventional management theory when he observed in 1993 that managers in the postcapitalist society will not be able to rely on command authority. Leaders and managers will be judged by the complexity of their jobs, the information they generate and use, and the kinds of relationships they establish to do their work, not by how many people report to them. In other words, the *linking* of workers rather than the *ranking* of workers will be an important criterion of success.[5]

Today the shape of organizations continues to change as increased competition both domestically and internationally forces massive layoffs and restructuring. The growing "externalization" of employment (i.e., the use of part-time employees, contract workers, and temporary help) is forcing executives to reassess the way they motivate, monitor, and evaluate employees.[6] And as organizational boundaries become more fluid and blurred, networking and collaboration play a greater role. Harvard Business School professor Rosabeth Kanter captures this new reality when she says, "Whatever the duration and objectives of business alliances, . . . in the global economy, a well-developed ability to create and sustain fruitful collaborations gives companies a significant competitive leg up."[7]

It seems obvious that organizations made up of alliances and networks would want managers who are comfortable sharing information. It seems obvious that organizations desiring more flexibility would want managers who are comfortable with ambiguity. It seems obvious that organizations striving for collaboration would want managers who view the redistribution of power as sharing, not surrendering. It seems obvious that organizations operating in an international context would want managers who appreciate cultural diversity. Since these are the leadership attributes I believe women display, it seems equally obvious that such organizations would turn to women managers. By and large, however, they do not. In early 1995—almost a decade after the *Wall Street Journal* made the term "glass ceiling" part of the business lexicon—the United States Glass Ceiling Commission reported that only 3 to 5 percent of senior U.S. executives were female.[8]

This statistic is stark evidence of an economic problem: the underutilization of women's leadership attributes. The basis for my assertion that women represent an untapped economic resource is their tendency to use a leadership style I call "interactive." In contrast to the command-and-control model, the interactive model emphasizes such attributes as consensus building, comfort with ambiguity, and the sharing of power and information. These attributes are increasingly recognized as critical to fast-changing, service-oriented, entrepreneurial, international organizations—the types of organizations best equipped to compete in the new global environment. In other words, I propose that there is a convergence between the need to reinvent today's organizations and the interactive leadership style of women.

If I am right, why hasn't this convergence been recognized? Why have so few women made it into the upper echelons of management? And why hasn't female underutilization been recognized as a bottom-line issue? I believe we can begin to answer these questions by looking at how organizations have addressed the issue of human resources in recent years.

People Who Need People

Good management has always been viewed as an important component of organizational success. There is no dearth of literature on leadership, motivation, and job enhancement. However, for the most part, current calls for change have been old wine in new bottles: articulate a vision, listen to your customers, delegate when possible, and control when necessary. Management thinking is still shaped by the pyramidal model of organizations, with a few sitting at the top and decisions flowing down. It is still generally assumed that organizations operate on the principle of meritocracy: those who merit promotions get promoted, and those at the top represent the greatest talent. Because this is taken for granted, the importance of leveraging talent has not been a major issue for executives. If the best people are automatically promoted and rise to positions of leadership, why be overly concerned with the effective use of human resources, much less female resources?

Although businesses and other organizations have not entirely overlooked the economic importance of human resources, they have rarely made it a top priority. Recently there has been a new concern about human resources, but it has focused mainly on the increasing diversity of America's future workforce and the shortage of skilled labor. For example, a widely cited 1987 study by the Hudson Institute predicted that by the year 2000, 85 percent of the net new entrants into the workforce would be women and people of color.[9] In 1988 *Business Week* published a special issue titled "Human Capital." The cover copy read in part, "The nation's ability to compete is threatened by inadequate investment in our most important resource: people."[10] Since then there has been a proliferation of articles highlighting the issue of cultural diversity in the workforce, but most have not linked it to organizational restructuring or the need for new kinds of leadership. In fact, many organizations view the composition of the newly diverse workforce as a problem rather than a resource.

A similar neglect of human resource utilization characterizes most theories of strategic management—that is, the models that help organizations develop competitive strategies. Until recently, none of these theories have paid much attention to leveraging human resources as a primary source of competitive advantage.

Traditionally, American management strategy has focused on domestic rather than international competition. As long as American products and services were considered top quality, U.S. businesses operated in a parochial manner, confining their overseas activities to opening new markets instead of increasing market share. Clearly, Japan's growing success in areas that had long been American strongholds should have been a warning to U.S. leaders that their business strategies needed revision. Instead, as Japan and other countries gained market share, the American business community called for government protection. It wasn't until the 1980s that serious attention was paid to the notion that the strategic management of most American firms was out of synch with the rapidly changing global marketplace.

In his 1980 best-seller, *Competitive Strategy,* Michael Porter outlined a model of strategic management that used a structural analysis of industries to assess their economic attractiveness.[11] Porter argued that firms could create a sustained competitive advantage and realize above-average profits by identifying structural market imperfections and capitalizing on them. Firms that chose to operate in structurally attractive industries would fare well, according to Porter, and those that didn't would not.

However, if industry structure is the major determinant of differences in competitive advantage, then why is there so much variation in the performance of firms within a given industry? This and other questions turn out to be better answered by the new resource-based theory of the firm, which emphasizes an organization's capabilities in relation to its competitors as the primary explanation for its performance.[12] Resource-based theory focuses on the value of building specialized asset combinations that create desirable, hard-to-imitate capabilities. The theory holds that an

Spiritual Gifts

organization's hard-to-imitate resources are a primary source of profit, and defines "resources" in a very general way. They can be nonhuman (technology, coal) or human (research expertise or what has been termed "economies of experience"). However, this model also sidesteps the issue of under-utilizing human resources.

The same is true of the thinking of "management's new gurus," who were the focus of a 1992 *Business Week* cover story.[13] "Business is hungry for fresh approaches to the global marketplace," said the article, which discussed such management theories as the learning organization (escaping linear thinking), reengineering (overhauling job design and organizing work around outcomes), core competencies (organizing around what a firm does best), organizational architecture (thinking about how work, people, and structures operate together), and time-based competition (time is money and therefore a source of competitive advantage). These theories have become popular with organizations attempting to gain a competitive edge. But despite their strengths, they suffer from the blind spot that afflicts resource-based theory and many other theories of strategic management: they ignore the importance of developing and leveraging the talents of the people in the organization.

In 1994 Stanford Business School professor Jeffrey Pfeffer argued that "the source of competitive advantage has always shifted over time," and that organizations and nations must now consider how they manage their workforce as the key to competitive advantage (an argument anticipated by Robert Reich, currently secretary of labor, in his 1991 *The Work of Nations*).[14] Thus, while strategic management issues such as economies of scale, access to financial resources, technological advances, industry-based distinctions, and the "new guru" theories have not been discarded, there is a new focus on people management.

Pfeffer's thinking is echoed by Ken Coleman, senior vice president of administration at Silicon Graphics, Inc., a $1.5 billion computer firm, who believes that the only real strategic weapon organizations have that can't be copied by their competition is their people.[15] There is a growing realization that improving an organization's bottom line in today's business environment requires the recognition and full utilization of all human resources, especially those previously ignored or overlooked. The implication is clear: firms that underutilize the talents of any of their employees, male or female, will find themselves at a competitive disadvantage.

Leadership and the Paradox of Gender

I don't think there's much doubt that the attributes and behaviors associated with women are those of the interactive leadership style. It would be simplistic and reductive to say that the interactive style is the exclusive province of women and the command-and-control style the exclusive province of men. All men do not behave in the same way, nor do all women. Clearly, gender differences exist along a continuum. But there is by now a large body of academic and popular literature suggesting that women and men do indeed tend to differ in the ways they think and act.[16] My own research has convinced me that these differences are real and that they carry over into leadership styles.

As early as 1978, in his famous book *Leadership*, James MacGregor Burns mentioned a male bias in the concept of leadership. He argued that leadership should be seen as a process in which leaders engaged and mobilized the human needs and aspirations of followers. When that happened, he said, women would be recognized as leaders and men would change their leadership style.[17] Tom Peters, author of the best-selling *In Search of Excellence*, makes reference in many of his syndicated newspaper columns to the effectiveness of female attributes in organizations that call for flexibility.

Cretin ?

10

Burns and Peters are exceptions in the leadership literature, however. A great deal has been written about the subject,[18] but most studies suggest that men and women display similar leadership traits, such as vision, intelligence, charisma, commitment, and drive. Male and female leaders look alike in this context because most leadership studies tend to focus on the traits themselves rather than how they are operationalized. Having observed female leaders, I was interested in testing the hypothesis that while men and women share general leadership traits, their leadership styles are quite different. I was convinced that those who had conducted leadership studies asked the wrong questions and looked in the wrong places for answers. They looked at large companies, large universities, and large government agencies. It might be expected that women leaders in these kinds of organizations would lead like men. In order to be promoted, they probably had to adopt the command-and-control leadership style. I wondered what happened to women (and men) who chose to lead in a different way. Where did they go? Did they succeed using a different leadership style?

In 1989, to answer these questions, I conducted a nationwide study of men and women leaders in diverse professions. In particular, I focused on a group of successful women leaders to ascertain how they exercised power, what kind of leadership style they preferred, and what kinds of organizations they worked in. As a basis for comparison, I looked at a similar group of male leaders at the same time. That study formed the basis of my article "Ways Women Lead," which was published in the *Harvard Business Review* in late 1990 and became a lightning rod for debate about gender differences in a management context.[19] I found that women, on average, exhibited and preferred the interactive leadership style, and men the command-and-control leadership style, and that the interactive style is particularly effective in flexible, nonhierarchical organizations of the kind that perform best in a climate of rapid change. My findings did not suggest that one style is better or worse than the other, only that men and women tend to lead differently and that interactive leaders tend to be most successful in nontraditional organizations.

As I have said, the inattention to human resource utilization in management thinking, along with the related assumption that "cream rises to the top," in part explains why organizations have not looked to women as leaders and why women are still so scarce in top management. However, I believe there is another factor at work, what I call the paradox of gender.

Paradox of Gender

—When attributes or behaviors associated with women are considered negative or of little value, gender is seen as relevant.

—When attributes or behaviors associated with women are considered positive or valuable, gender is seen as irrelevant.

As long as the command-and-control management style dominated organizations, female-linked behaviors such as consensus building, power sharing, and comfort with ambiguity were considered signs of weakness, and gender was the explanation. These behaviors, judged wanting in comparison to the command-and-control style, were supposedly what made women unfit for leadership roles. But as doubts about the effectiveness of the command-and-control model made their way into the executive suite, these same behaviors began to appear in a positive light and were no longer considered female. They were now simply good leadership traits. It is revealing, for example, that in defending the role of intuition and emotion in management decisions, Herbert Simon made no mention of the prevailing view of these qualities as "female" and therefore irrational and unreliable. Similarly, when the attributes associated with the interactive leadership style are considered organizationally effective, they are often presented as gender-neutral. Ironically, in some organizations men are now being trained to be interactive leaders while women are still hitting the glass ceiling because they *are* interactive leaders.

Two Stories

If you saw her walking down the street, you would never guess Raydean Acevedo is the owner and chief executive officer of a profitable $23 million corporation that employs 280 workers. This petite young Latina started and remains the sole owner of Research Management Consultants, Inc. (RMCI), a company that provides environmental engineering, information systems, telecommunications, architectural and industrial services, research, and training to commercial firms and government agencies. Acevedo's career path could not have been predicted. Now forty-three, she holds a degree in sociology from the University of California, Santa Barbara. She wasn't sure how she would apply her knowledge, but she never expected to have her own business.

Acevedo started her career as a sociologist doing what she calls her "social science thing," training and research for ABT Associates in Washington, D.C. A former colleague at ABT recruited her to work in a Fortune 500 corporation where she would be responsible for selling and marketing optical mark reader systems and services (OMRs). The move would require her to learn a great deal of technical information about OMRs in addition to becoming a manager.

Acevedo refers jokingly to the "corporate interview gauntlet" she ran before being offered the job. She knew she would have to master OMRs. She knew she would be managing others. She expected questions that would be difficult for someone with no previous training or experience in sales, much less in selling computer hardware. She felt confident of her answers until the last interviewer of the day asked, "How are you at closing?" Acevedo didn't understand what he meant, but she lost little time in replying. "If I open them, I close them!" she said. She got the job, and she's been closing them ever since.

She was an immediate success at the new corporation. <u>She made customers feel important</u>. <u>She was quick to respond to their needs</u>. She was <u>not afraid to ask questions</u> of her technical colleagues, and s<u>he was a good listener</u>. She sh<u>ared information and power</u>, and was <u>generous with praise</u>. She was comfortable with her managerial style although it was different from that of her male colleagues. And yet she always felt like an outsider because she was a woman. Acevedo was not included in the "old boys' network" even though her male colleagues clearly respected her performance. She knew she was viewed as different. She became a workaholic in an effort to win acceptance.

Acevedo knew she could market and sell, and it didn't take long to learn what she needed to know about the company's products. She enrolled in night courses at the local community college to develop her data-processing expertise. The company's major corporate competitor was aware of her success and tried to hire her away. She was hesitant, not sure of the social and professional propriety of "jumping ship" to join the competition. The competitor firm did not give up. They acquired her division—the only way they could get Acevedo, some of her colleagues joked. However, she still felt like an outsider in the new organization.

Acevedo started reading books like *Games Mother Never Taught You* in hopes of learning how to be "one of the boys." Nothing she read or did worked. She kept wondering how she might change her behavior. "Is my management style getting in the way of my being accepted?" she asked herself. "Am I really the problem? Why don't I fit in?" Although she continued to receive promotions and pay increases, the realization that she was "different" bothered her. Her male boss often made sexist remarks and teased her about being inferior because she was a woman. She tried to ignore his behavior and do her job, but she constantly felt on the defensive. Her boss told her repeatedly that he found her performance outstanding, but then he would say, "I don't know how to treat you." Once he even told her, "I don't know who you remind me of most—my wife or my daughter. At times you drive me nuts, but I still love you. It's like when my daughter does something wrong. I have to punish her because I care." Acevedo's boss didn't talk that way to his male managers, and she began to realize that he didn't know how to interact with a woman in a professional environment. He related to her as a woman in a traditional female role. No matter what she did, she would never be one of the boys.

Still she worked harder, trying to make up for not being male by being helpful to her boss and male colleagues. Unfortunately, her efforts were often met with ridicule. Once, she approached a male supervisor who was about to testify before a key congressional committee. Acevedo had worked on community activities with the committee chairman, who was a Latino. She knew him well. She offered to introduce her supervisor to the chairman, thinking this would help her company's credibility. She felt she was offering something important—her personal reputation—and was surprised at the response: "You can accompany me to the hearing if you want, but you'll have to sit in the front row and unbutton the top two buttons of your blouse." This comment really hurt. Acevedo had made a serious suggestion, but the supervisor could see her only in the context of her sexuality. She went home in despair, convinced that the company would never accept her for who she was.

These incidents took their emotional toll. When one of Acevedo's customers asked if she had ever thought of starting her own business, she began to wonder. She knew she was competent. She also knew she was being paid a lower base salary than her male counterparts (one of whom she had hired and trained). True, she made a higher total income, but that was because she earned bonuses for her successful sales. It was now clear to her that if she were to make it to the executive suite, she would have to find her own way there.

In her first and subsequent jobs, Acevedo experienced a phenomenon familiar to many professional women, and to minorities as well, something called competency testing. Over and over again she had to convince those with whom she worked that she was competent. She had to put in extra-long hours, she had to produce more than anyone else doing the same job, and most important, she had to show she could "fit in." Men also have to work hard and produce. But men—particularly white men—are assumed to be competent until they prove their incompetence. Women are assumed to be incompetent and continually have to prove otherwise—doubly so if they are minority women like Acevedo.

Acevedo hadn't considered starting her own business until her customer suggested it. She had been told there were incentives for women to start businesses, so she decided to pursue the possibility. She did some investigating, talked to lots of people, and worked nonstop to develop a business plan and assure capital to cover her start-up costs and cash flow. Then she took the plunge. She joined the ranks of women jumping from large corporations into the entrepreneurial pool. The rest is history. Today her award-winning firm generates new jobs for U.S. workers, provides new sources of private sector revenue, and utilizes the talents that were wasted by a company that couldn't see past her gender.

Mary Midyette's story is different but equally informative. Her letter of resignation from a multibillion-dollar railroad corporation says it all.[20]

> I have been a loyal and successful sales representative . . . for twelve years, but I am tired of fighting the battle. Once I believed it was worth it; fighting the "token woman" image, biting my tongue at innuendoes and jokes, . . . and trying to prove my worthiness (earning an M.B.A. and working steadily through two pregnancies and returning to work six weeks

after both, even though one was a Cesarean section). I firmly believed that this company would recognize and reward hard work.

Midyette's letter explained that she stopped believing in the company when she applied for a managerial sales position that was given to a man who was clearly less qualified. Insulted and furious, she complained about being passed over and was told that the man who got the job was a friend of the boss.

To appease her, Midyette's boss told her of an opportunity in another department. He said it was a new position that would involve the managerial responsibility she sought. Since the position had just been created, she understood it might take time to clarify her role, but she accepted the transfer. Midyette didn't want to move out of sales, where she was a star performer, but she did want a management opportunity. While waiting for an office, she worked in the firm's marketing library for several months with no

"You both are my two best employees . . ." Reprinted by permission Tribune Media Services.

no legal or paragraph authority

phone or desk. <u>Finally she realized there was no corporate commitment to the new position</u>. It was then that she tendered her resignation. The final paragraph of her resignation letter is particularly instructive.

> Maybe if I could look to some women role models in this company, I could hang on. But where are they? They do not exist. I predict the company will continue to see a pattern of defection by women, taking their knowledge and wisdom with them. Get smart. Value diversity and hold on to it dearly. It, more than anything else, can carry you into the next century.

Midyette's background had clearly prepared her for a managerial career. She graduated from William and Mary College with a degree in business administration. She worked as a sales trainee at a large railroad company. Like Acevedo, she was promoted rapidly but was paid less than her male counterparts. She earned an M.B.A., thinking it would speed her advancement, but the degree and the knowledge it represented were ignored. Many of the men with whom Midyette worked didn't have college degrees, and she realized they might envy her education.

When Midyette was pregnant with her first child in 1985, she didn't tell her boss. In her own words, she felt she would have been "dead in the water" if she had. Eventually, she had to tell him. He turned beet red and didn't know what to say or do. He made it difficult for Midyette to feel happy about becoming a mother. In fact, he made her feel she had done something wrong. The company's maternity policy required women to return to work six weeks after giving birth, so although she had a Cesarean, major surgery, she didn't request extra time off. She thought this would show her commitment to the firm.

Today Midyette recalls many other distressing incidents. Once, she attended a company golf tournament and was asked to drive the "alcohol cart," a little car that followed the players (all male) with cold beer. "How insulting," she thought, and refused. At the dinner after the tournament one of her male peers asked mockingly, "Should I pull out your chair?"—as though courtesy might bother her because she was a professional woman. Then a corporate executive began the dinner program with, "Welcome, gentlemen—oh, sorry, I mean lady too." The day was capped by a kiss on the forehead, accompanied by, "Little Mary, I always knew you were special, you're just so cute!"

Initially, Midyette did not tie all these incidents together. It had never occurred to her that being female was preventing her from achieving her career goals. It was her husband who finally "turned on the light." One day, while they were in the company elevator together, he noticed that Midyette's male co-workers talked to each other but didn't acknowledge her presence. It was as though she didn't exist. Later he said to her, "How are you ever going to get ahead in this company? They're never going to accept you."

When Midyette finally resigned in late 1992, there was only one woman in upper management in the entire company, and that woman was in a staff position. Learning of Midyette's departure, other women with whom she had previously had little interaction called to share similar stories of being devalued and underutilized. There was shock and disbelief among the men when Midyette resigned. This was a company that promoted from within, a company where loyalty was valued and employees rarely left.

While Midyette never thought much about it at the time, she realized after leaving the firm that her experience symbolized a pervasive problem for women. They are often devalued, taken for granted, and underutilized. Midyette is now working in a company where she is appreciated and advancing rapidly. Her present employer is profiting from her expertise. Her former company has suffered a loss.

The stories of Raydean Acevedo and Mary Midyette illustrate what I mean when I describe the untapped potential of America's professional women as a secret: not that this potential has purposely been ignored but that it has been hidden from view. Certainly, it was hidden from the companies Acevedo and Midyette left. No one denies that the discrimination women experience in the workplace by virtue of being women is a social equity issue. That's no secret. But the fact that women constitute an economic resource that can provide a competitive advantage is very much a secret. In most organizations it has yet to be discovered.

Are men threatened?

What about Tomorrow?

If at least 95 percent of top executive positions are held by men, either there are very few women worthy of holding such positions or competent women are being overlooked. We know it's not the first case, since there is a large cadre of well-educated, experienced professional women in the United States. That leaves us with the second case: for some reason, the talents of these women are being underutilized.

What I am suggesting is that despite the new appreciation for the interactive leadership style and the increasing emphasis on the importance of human resource utilization, the paradox of gender prevents organizations from seeing the huge untapped pool of women leaders that is in plain sight. Focusing on market share, structural change, organizational learning, job redesign, etc., is necessary but no longer sufficient. Paying attention to gender differences has become an economic imperative. Organizations that ignore the competitive advantage women represent do so at their own peril.

A few organizations are beginning to link the gender debate with economic competitiveness. In many instances, however, this development has less to do with an appreciation for women as leaders than with a heightened awareness of women as a customer base. Clearly, as more women become lawyers, doctors, CPAs, and professors, they constitute an important market for all types of good and services. No longer can Cadillac and Lexus dealers assume they will be selling their cars only to men (though female sales managers are still rare in the automobile business). Infiniti has launched a major campaign targeting women consumers. "Who's buying most of the cars in this country?" asks a recent ad, and supplies the answer.

> Conventional wisdom might lead you to believe that most car buyers are men. But Infiniti believes in the importance of tracking trends and mastering the marketplace. By the year 2000, nearly 60% of all cars sold will be purchased by women. Today women purchase 47% of all cars bought and significantly influence 90% of all purchases. Infiniti takes this trend seriously. "We make women feel welcome at local dealers through programs designed specifically for these influential car buyers," says Deborah Thayer, Infiniti's Creative/Media Manager.[21]

As female preferences become larger determinants of consumer behavior, companies realize that women executives must be given a role in deciding how products and services should be designed and marketed. No longer can law and CPA firms assume that their clients will be male or that only men will decide what firm should represent their organization in court or handle their taxes. No longer can advertising agencies assume that it will be only men who decide what ad campaign to approve. No longer can consultants assume that it will be only men who decide who gets a contract. Therefore, organizations must recognize that they need the decision-making talents of women not only as a tool for capturing the women's market but as a way to make themselves more competitive.

Some leading-edge executives have become convinced that recruiting and retaining professional women is a top priority. For example, Deloitte & Touche, a large public accounting firm, is in the midst of a major Women's Initiative. According to CEO J. Michael Cook, it is their number one human resource effort. When questioned about its necessity, as he often is, he says, "First, it is the right thing to do. We promise young people a career in which they have the opportunity to succeed to the full extent of their abilities, and this promise must be unequivocal for everybody." Second, Cook says that a professional services business like Deloitte & Touche needs the very best people if it is to deliver the highest quality of service. Today, 40 percent of the firm's client services professionals and 50 percent of those it hires are women.[22]

Hardwick Simmons, president and CEO of Prudential Securities, also sees women as a resource that must be better utilized if his firm is to keep its competitive edge. "I believe women are well suited for sales and leadership positions in the securities business," he says. "Investors are looking more and more for a relationship with their financial advisers. They want someone they can trust, someone who listens. I don't know if it's nature or nurture, but in my experience, in general, women may be better at these kinds of relationship-building skills than are men. Candidly, I think there's no way for a firm to win in our business in the future without tapping into these skills."[23]

Diane McGarry, an American who runs the Canadian branch of Xerox, characterized the appointment of Maureen Kempston Darkes as head of General Motors in Canada as "the wake-up call for companies to take out their organization charts and spot people who can be developed."[24] Another Xerox manager, Dr. Rafik Loutfy, vice president of the Xerox Research Centre of Canada, told me he had noticed that the men in his operation always seemed to be at war, something he attributed to their socialization. The women, on the other hand, seemed more flexible and more willing to adapt to change. As a result of his observations, Dr. Loutfy began to appreciate the "female way of doing things" as a special human resource. Now he actively seeks out women as potential leaders in the Research Centre.[25]

Perhaps the clearest affirmation that women constitute

an underutilized economic resource comes from John Collins, former chairman and chief executive of Shell U.K. In a memo to employees he wrote, "For too long macho management has been hailed as the only way to run things, and that has put women at a disadvantage, with their abilities measured against criteria set by men. This has been a tremendous waste of talent—something that business can no longer afford."[26]

Where Do We Go from Here?

This book is organized on the principle of enlightened self-interest. The chapters are designed to help organizations see the link between fully utilizing the talents of their professional women and improving their bottom line.

Most organizations are guided by a "one best model" associated with white male values, attitudes, and behaviors. Coupled with this is a mind-set that views difference from the best model pejoratively. Chapter 2 explores these two mind-sets and shows how they contribute to the underutilization of women and thereby diminish organizational effectiveness.

Although there is general agreement about what "underutilization" means, there is little agreement about how to measure it. Chapter 3 describes five objective measures that support the contention that professional women in the United States are underutilized.

Numerous theories have been advanced to explain gender differences and account for female underutilization. I have my own theory about the underutilization of women, one I call "sexual static"—the irritation and discomfort men feel working with women in new roles when there are no agreed-upon new rules. Sexual static is explained in Chapter 4.

Men are used to supervising women, but only recently have they worked with women as peers, competitors, and bosses. Chapter 5 discusses men's feelings about these new relationships and the relevance of their feelings to female underutilization.

Women are used to feeling underutilized and devalued at work. But how do they translate these feelings into reactions and behavior? Chapter 6 provides some answers.

When women assume positions of power in organizations, they create changes in male and female behavior, power relationships, decision processes, and organizational agendas. The impact of these changes is the subject of Chapter 7.

Before organizations can leverage the special talents of women, they have to receive a wake-up call that convinces them of the need to do so. Chapter 8 discusses reactions to the wake-up call and outlines the various stages of gender awareness in which organizations find themselves. It also shows the similarity of these stages to stages of organizational awareness about the need to restructure, and clarifies the symbiotic relationship between restructuring and more fully utilizing the talents of women.

Chapter 9 describes the process of change as organizations move from one stage of awareness to another. It suggests specific ways of generating change, presents a detailed cycle of change, and follows one Fortune 500 company as it goes through the cycle.

For organizations that still haven't received the wake-up call, Chapter 10 may do the trick. It offers a comparative survey of the underutilization of women in the United States, Britain, Japan, and the European Union. The results suggest that many of America's global competitors are beginning to realize the value of their professional women in economic terms. In Britain, female underutilization is the focus of several important initiatives, and the European Union has held a number of major conferences on the issue. And while Japan and other Asian countries are far behind the United States in matters of gender equality, the absolute number of Asian women, if and when they follow the path taken by American women, could produce a resource pool that would greatly alter America's ability to compete.

It's time for U.S. organizations to act. It's time for them to discover a rich economic resource that can be tapped at very little cost—a resource unique to America. No other country in the world has a comparable supply of professional women waiting to be called into action. *This* is America's competitive secret.

2

The One Best Model

When you scan the business section of the bookstores, one thing becomes clear. The best-sellers are usually corporate success stories or narratives about colorful leaders. They explicitly or implicitly point to an organizational structure or a leadership style felt to be the pathway to success. The message these books send is that there is "one best model," one best way to design and run an organization and one best way to lead. It's a seductive message.

The desire for a single best answer is understandable. It satisfies the need to simplify and the longing for certainty. It offers order in place of chaos. It makes planning seem possible. It justifies past actions. Most important, it calms fears, reinforces deeply held values, and removes the burden of figuring out what to do. But it also masks real problems and discounts alternative approaches to the complicated matter of how best to structure and lead an organization.

It took Bernard Bass 914 information-packed pages to discuss various leadership theories in one of the most authoritative books ever written on the subject.[1] Those who take the time to read Bass's classic work and reflect on its meaning soon discover that it is a grave mistake to assume there is one best leadership model. Bass's analysis of leadership teaches that

> the extent to which one leadership style is effective compared to alternative styles depends on the environment and organization in which the leadership is enacted, on the immediate group of followers, on the characteristics of the task, on spatial arrangements and networks, on how much stress is being generated and on whether substitutes for leadership exist in the situation.[2]

What model or combination of model works for us?

Nonetheless, most organizations tend to reward the command-and-control leadership style, and are still dominated by a belief that there is one right way of doing things—*their* way. This is what I call the one-best-model mind-set.

As we saw in the last chapter, the effectiveness of traditional leadership models and organizational structures has periodically been questioned. Unfortunately, the belief that there is one best model seems to be stronger than doubts about the effectiveness of any particular model. Consider the groundswell of enthusiasm for the Japanese model of management that swept the United States in the early 1980s, when books like W. M. Ouchi's *Theory Z* tapped into a growing sense of unease about America's ability to compete in the global marketplace.[3] The initial infatuation abated when it became apparent that the Japanese management style was more top-down than had been thought and that it was embedded in a culture quite different from America's. But this disenchantment did not extend to the impulse to find another new model and apply it lock, stock, and barrel as a panacea. Organizations are still driven by a search for one best answer.

The yearning for one best model persists today as organizations rush to embrace the latest restructuring trend or the management theory of the month. It is this desire for easy answers to complex problems that has made benchmarking, for example, so popular. Benchmarking involves identifying one or more companies as the best in some category (leadership, production, marketing, recruiting and retaining women, etc.) and then using those companies as a performance standard. Benchmarking minimizes the discomfort organizations must face when they examine their policies. It is thought to provide a prescription for what ails them. However, because it rests on the belief that there is one best way to do things, benchmarking often fosters a copycat mentality that can be counterproductive. What is best for one organization is not necessarily best for another, even when they are in the same industry. Rarely are two organizations the same.

The comments of an executive who talked to me on an airplane illustrate this point.[4] He is the CEO of a mid-sized computer manufacturing firm. He told me he had a gut feeling that there was too much cultural diversity in his firm because his employees seemed to argue all the time. Wanting to improve his firm's efficiency, he looked at successful companies and noticed the homogeneity of their thinking. He was particularly impressed with Wal-Mart and decided to copy its way of doing things—that is, to use Wal-Mart as a benchmark. When I suggested to him that effective strategies for a company that sells discount prescriptions and household items would probably not work the same way in a company that sells high-technology computers, he scratched his head. It hadn't occurred to him that while homogeneity might be appropriate in an operation where standardization was important, a variety of ideas and approaches was needed to create sophisticated computer hardware.

This executive had been looking for an answer to a poorly phrased question. Rather than asking where he could find one best model to emulate, he should have asked how to capitalize on the different insights and ideas his arguing employees were expressing.

Command-and-Control as the One Best Model

In the context of American management, the one best model has traditionally been the command-and-control model. Organizations using this model are hierarchical and have clear lines of authority. Decisions are made from the top down, and it is assumed that those at the top know best. Performance is judged on individual rather than group contribution, and criteria for advancement have as much to do with fitting in as with competence. As its name suggests, the command-and-control model strongly resembles the military. It is no surprise that books about military leaders like Norman Schwarzkopf and Colin Powell, and corporate CEOs like Ross Perot and Lee Iacocca, are popular with businessmen. Their stories and philosophies reinforce the belief that success comes from being a commanding male manager.

American institutions tend to look alike. They have similar structures and practices, and similar kinds of leaders.[5] Typically, American executives are white, male, heterosexual, and married with children. They are individualists, linear thinkers, sports fans, and usually military veterans. They also tend to be workaholics and graduates of prestigious colleges. They value their families but spend little time with them.[6] Although there are many women who aspire to and are qualified for positions of power in major organizations, female leaders remain the exception rather than the rule. As Julie Newcomb Hill, CEO of Costain Homes, has said, "There's only so much shelf space for women at the top of organizations."[7]

Given the success of American institutions in the past, it can't be denied that the command-and-control model worked. And because white males created and led most organizations, it isn't surprising that they occupy the most powerful positions. But as Yogi Berra said years ago, "The

"Actually, Lou, I think it was more than just my being in the right place at the right time. I think it was my being the right race, the right religion, the right sex, the right socioeconomic group, having the right accent, the right clothes, going to the right schools . . ."

"Actually Lou, I think . . . " Drawing by W. Miller; © 1992 *The New Yorker Magazine*, Inc.

future ain't what it used to be." The economic climate has changed, and organizations and theories of management must change too. As noted earlier, it has become apparent that the command-and-control model does not always produce optimal results.

However, to say that command-and-control leadership is no longer the one best model is not to say that it has lost its value. It has not. Rather, it is to say that there *is* no one best model, and that command-and-control leadership is only *one of many models* that can help an organization compete in today's work environment.

Increasingly, what I have described as the interactive

leadership model is seen as desirable and complementary to the command-and-control model. The interactive style involves managing in a collaborative rather than top-down fashion. It is characterized by the use of a reward system that values group as well as individual contributions, the empowerment of workers at all levels, multidirectional feedback and performance evaluation, and a strong emphasis on interpersonal as well as technical skills. This style is well suited to fast-changing organizations that require flexibility, individual and group self-direction, and comfort with the sharing of power and information. It is the style many professional women tend to prefer. Yet because it differs from the male command-and-control style, women have not been viewed as potential leaders. Instead they have been the target of books advising them that if they want to succeed, they have to think and act like men.[8] Implicit in this idea is the assumption that the "right" or "best" way to run an organization is the white male way.

Over time, women develop a particular set of skills and values shaped by their life experiences. For example, they are comfortable with ambiguity because their lives are full of uncertainty. They are good at juggling and completing many tasks simultaneously because that is the story of their daily existence. It isn't strange to see a woman feeding a baby, watching the news on TV, listening to her husband, and thinking about how to solve a problem at work, all at the same time. Not so with men, who more often than not have the luxury of focusing on one or two things at a time. It is not strange for women to change plans and moods as often as sheets, because household chores and family responsibilities are not easily scheduled and women rarely have others to take care of their schedules for them. Women simultaneously have to satisfy the different needs and conflicting demands of husbands, parents, in-laws, children, friends, and fellow workers. Consequently, they develop negotiating skills that are often different from those of men.

The way 'brains' are wired

31

I am not suggesting that men do not also experience ambiguity and conflicting demands. Henry Mintzberg, in *The Nature of Managerial Work*, points out that the daily experience of men is punctuated with interruptions.[9] However, most male executives resent interruptions and often use their secretaries to shield them from distractions. Women executives tend not to see unscheduled tasks and encounters as unwelcome interruptions but rather as opportunities to connect.[10] And men generally do not have to juggle household chores with managerial work responsibilities, whereas most professional women work a "second shift" that never goes away.[11]

This second-shift responsibility, along with women's tendency to speak "in a different voice" and "women's ways of knowing," differentiates them from their male colleagues at work.[12] These differences, in my opinion, help explain why women never fully measure up to the standards of the one best model and thus are seen as less competent than men.

Most management experts agree that today's organizations call for leaders who can wear more than one hat and work well in an unpredictable environment where power relationships are not always clear or stable. It seems to me that because of their life experience, women are well prepared for leadership in this kind of environment. Dr. Rafik Loutfy of the Xerox Research Centre in Canada shares this view.

> Senior management in corporate America is driven by decisions based on information collected and filtered through a mental framework. An unchanging, rigid framework is responsible for the demise of many onetime successful businesses. Conversely, a constantly changing mental perspective is required to succeed in a rapidly changing business environment. Women, through years of coping with diverse life demands, have developed a greater ability to constantly adapt their mental perspective and are able to draw on a large set of different perspectives at once—an ability that is required for corporate success in the future.[13]

Difference as Deficiency

The one-best-model mentality goes hand in hand with another entrenched mind-set, one already implied. It is a mind-set that sees difference as deficiency, deviance, or dysfunction. That is, whenever we notice that one thing is different from another, we ask, "Is it better or worse?" As defined in the dictionary, "difference" means "the condition of not being the same in quality." The word "difference," then, inherently suggests a measurement based on some standard. And if the standard is considered "best," it follows that those who differ from it can only be "worse." The one-best-model mind-set makes it impossible to view the state of being different positively.

The experience of most career women, whether they like to admit it or not, is that being viewed as different has meant being viewed as deficient or deviant. No matter how many college degrees they earn, no matter how many hours they work, no matter how they dress or how good their golf game is, they don't seem to have the right stuff. When the standard of quality is male, being a woman means being less good. When women point out this dilemma, a typical male reaction is that women want it both ways—to be seen as different from men yet to be treated the same as men. But is this so? Women don't want to be treated like men. They just don't want to be devalued or seen as less competent because they're different from men.

The dilemma is difficult for men to understand because the two mind-sets I have been discussing are deeply rooted in the workplace culture. As a result, men do not recognize that they subconsciously see women as less able than themselves.

Of course, the workplace doesn't exist in a vacuum. We live in a society that also operates on a one best model associated with white males. The scarcity of women at the top of almost all American institutions, whether in business, education, government, religion, or the military, sends a message that women don't belong in leadership positions. Although there has been some progress in recent years, it is still news when a woman is elected governor or U.S. senator, named as CEO of a major corporation, promoted to general in the army, or ordained in a mainline religion. Everywhere we turn, women are climbing organizational ladders but getting stuck along the way.

There are many examples of how the one-best-model mind-set manifests itself in the workplace. One need only listen to people talk about their "woman doctor," "black lawyer," or "gay CPA." Such phrases imply that doctors, lawyers, and CPAs are not supposed to be female, black, or gay. People don't say they're seeing a male doctor or a white lawyer or a straight CPA. It's assumed all professionals are white males, so when one is not, a special description seems warranted.

Ask most professional women if they are evaluated by the same standards as their male counterparts and they will say no. They will point to the fact that having a family is a plus for male executives and a minus for female executives. Being aggressive is a plus for men and a minus for women. Being participative has recently become a plus for men but is still seen as a managerial weakness for women. Female professionals labor under the constraints of the one best model every working day, and consistently feel devalued and underutilized.

In an informal survey, I asked approximately a hundred male and female managers, "Do you feel the under-utilization of employees differs depending on the sex of the employee?"[14] Most of the women said yes and most of the men said no. Anecdotes that accompanied the yes answers were informative. The women said their management style and performance were valued less than men's even though they were just as productive. They said they felt devalued on two levels in particular: personal and organizational.

Devaluation on a Personal Level

On a personal level, the experience of being devalued takes many forms. There are subtle attitudes and behaviors that chip away at a woman's self-esteem. Even praise for a woman's competence may make her feel like an anomaly, because it is often expressed in a tone of surprise. And as noted above, references to a "woman dentist" or a "woman accountant" don't go unnoticed. They too suggest that women don't belong in a male profession.

Female academics point out that their secretaries often call male faculty members "professor" or "doctor" but call them by their first names. Since words both structure and reflect the way people think, the use of their first names makes women professors feel that their work is taken less seriously than that of male professors. The women don't object to being called by their first names, but they feel the same informality should be used with male professors so the status issue is eliminated.

It isn't just words that make women feel devalued. Each day as a woman gets dressed for work, she faces a problem men don't face: what to wear. Men need only decide among suits that are gray, brown, blue, or black, shirts that are usually white, and ties, which are their one chance to look different. The point is that their choices have to do mainly with colors. Women have to make much more complicated choices. If a woman wears a short skirt, she may be viewed as unprofessional. If she wears a V-neck blouse, she may be accused of tempting the boss to look down it. If she wears a tailored suit, she may be thought too masculine. What to wear is a difficult issue for women. They constantly have to walk the fine line between looking feminine and looking professional. In other words, women have to consider the sexual aspects of their clothing; men do not.

Sarah Warmington is a case in point. A prominent CPA, she was one of the few women in her firm. One day the executive secretary to the managing partner invited Warmington to a "trunk show"—a fashion presentation where designers bring clothes in a trunk and those who attend have an opportunity to try them on and purchase them. The show was "by invitation only," and Warmington was flattered that the secretary asked her to go. She accepted, happy to have an opportunity to develop a relationship with another woman in the firm, since there were so few.

Warmington is very attractive and in her late thirties. She is married and interested in clothes as well as accounting. Her clothes are fashionable and trendy, yet certainly not "cheap" or noticeably sexy. The suits and dresses at the trunk show seemed conventional to Warmington, but she tried on one that she liked. She thought the skirt was too long and asked if it could be shortened. The secretary seemed quite concerned and said to Warmington, "You don't really want to shorten that skirt, do you? If you shorten it, you won't look professional." Warmington looked at her quizzically and asked, "Are you on a mission?"

The next day Warmington confronted the managing partner, who had previously made some offhand remarks about her clothes being too sexy. At the time she had ignored his comments, but now a lightbulb went on. He had asked his executive secretary to give her advice about her clothes. Hence the trunk show invitation! Warmington rightly asked what her clothing had to do with her performance as a CPA. The fact that the managing partner was judging her on her physical appearance rather than her intellectual ability made Warmington feel devalued.[15] This is a common experience for professional women.

A dramatic illustration of judging by appearances was recorded by clinicians at the University of Minnesota Medical School. According to their report, men who had sex-change operations to become women claimed they had lost twenty IQ points on the operating table. Conversely, a thirty-six-year-old San Francisco secretary said she learned all about gender and credibility after she had a sex-change operation to become a man: "All of a sudden, once I was a male, everything I said was brilliant. I got a promotion, a title and a secretary of my own."[16] These stories provide powerful evidence that women are perceived as less credible than men merely because they are female and differ from the one best model.

Devaluation on an Organizational Level

Not only do women feel devalued on a personal level, they feel devalued because of organizational policies and practices that inherently disadvantage them. The difference-as-deficiency mind-set is built into most organizations and colors the way they handle such matters as titles and promotions, task assignments, meeting formats, benefit packages, and reward systems.

Sharon Timmer's experience at a large cosmetics firm in 1975 illustrates how deep-seated organizational insensitivity to women's talents can be. Although 1975 may seem a long time ago, similar experiences are heard whenever professional women get together. Timmer is a very talented marketing executive who was recruited by the cosmetics firm for a high-level position that involved major marketing responsibilities. When it came time to discuss her title, she was told not to expect a vice presidency. "Why not?" she asked. The answer was straightforward: "We already have a female vice president."[17]

This reply may seem farfetched, but one look at the annual reports of major American corporations reveals that not much has changed in the last two decades. When you look from the top down, there appear to be lots of women; when you look from the bottom up, you wonder why women are so scarce. Most large organizations still have few women vice presidents, and those few are almost always in staff rather than line positions, meaning that they lack budgetary and decision-making authority. There are many women who qualify for vice president positions, but they don't receive them because of the subconscious notion that to be a vice president is to be male.

As Sharon Timmer discovered, even when women do make it to the top, they are often victims of "tokenism," a phenomenon discussed at length by Professor Rosabeth Moss Kanter in *Men and Women of the Corporation*.[18] Token women—the only women in a sea of men—shoulder burdens that men don't have to carry. They are particularly visible and easily scrutinized. Their behavior is interpreted as representative of all women. Their presence challenges the value of sameness but at the same time reinforces the commonality of men. The token woman is both an insider and an outsider and has to walk a high wire between being female and being one of the boys. In other words, she has a hard row to hoe.

A few years ago, an oilman in Texas was proudly showing me his oil fields and the extensive empire he had built. Knowing I was in town to talk about women and work, he told me how supportive his firm was of its women employees. I asked him if he had ever hired a woman as a supervisor in his fields. He looked at me as though I had asked the right question, and said, "Yes, I hired a woman from Texas A and M and put her in charge of one of my field operations, but she didn't work out." He seemed to feel he had tried and that was that. When I asked if he had ever hired a man who didn't work out, he replied, "Of course!" A perplexed look came over his face as he realized what he had said. When a man didn't work out, he hired another man. When the token woman he hired didn't work out, he decided women couldn't do the job.

In addition to tokenism, women are frequently assigned tasks different from those of men, based on preconceived notions of what women want to or are able to do. For example, law and CPA firms often assume that women don't want assignments that require them to work late at night in downtown urban areas, to travel a great deal, or, in the case of law, to litigate. Women are not always consulted about whether they want such assignments. Then they find that since they have not done the "tough jobs," they are considered less experienced than the men who have.

There is increasing acknowledgment that disparity in assignments works against women.[19] One respondent to my survey questionnaire said, "When a man is an administrative assistant, he is frequently given analytic work to do. Female administrative assistants are usually given clerical work, even though they are as capable of doing analytic work as the men." A woman in a large management consulting company said that women in her firm are treated as advisers while men with the same titles and similar responsibilities are treated as sales executives. In other words, the women are seen as support personnel and the men are seen as "rainmakers," even when the women are bringing in the same number of clients as the men. These organizational perceptions, my respondent wrote, have "tremendous financial implications when it comes to bonuses."

Valerie O'Donnell knows about differential task assignments from her experience at a West Coast law firm. O'Donnell received her law degree in 1984 from the University of Birmingham in England. She moved to the United States several years later and worked in a major law firm on the East Coast where she was responsible for all mergers and acquisitions. Well respected in the firm, she was noted for closing some large transactions, and earned a reputation as a competent attorney in the field of corporate law. A California firm that specialized in mergers and acquisitions repeatedly tried to hire her. She was hesitant to move but finally accepted the offer. When she arrived in California in 1990, there were no women partners, but she expected that to change.

After several years at the firm, O'Donnell began to notice that the male attorneys always seemed to get the best cases, although assignments were supposed to be based on expertise and experience. The men were given litigation responsibilities, and having litigation work under your belt meant the difference between making or not making partner. O'Donnell suspected that the partners assigned men to help them on the big cases because they preferred working with men. She noticed she was not being assigned cases she felt qualified to handle. She had heard about how the "boys' club" worked, and now it seemed to her that she was seeing it in action. Her feeling was confirmed when she overheard one partner say to another, after a Department of Labor seminar on sexual harassment, "The way to solve this harassment problem is to limit the number of women we have around here." The partner's remark was an attempt to dismiss women by wrapping them in sexual trappings. The organizational climate was one that made female lawyers feel like second-class citizens as the question of ability was lost in the men's discomfort working with them as peers.

O'Donnell's frustration deepened when the firm decided to open an office in London, where the partners had few contacts. The mergers and acquisitions business in England is quite different from the U.S. brand. O'Donnell, who had practiced in London before she moved to America, had numerous contacts there. She offered to meet with her colleague who would be heading the London office, but he wasn't interested. She's sure that had she been male, her offer would have been accepted.[20]

Many women experience such slights on a regular basis, during meetings in which suggestions made by women are ignored until a man voices them. This is such a common occurrence that it is featured in many training videos designed to raise awareness of sexual discrimination in work settings. Moreover, meetings are often conducted in structured ways that inhibit women, who tend to be much less formal and more interactive.

The devaluation of women on an organizational level is also apparent in the benefit packages and perks offered key employees and executives. Despite considerable evi-

"THAT'S AN EXCELLENT SUGGESTION, MS WINTHROP?
WE'LL WAIT FOR ONE OF THE MEN HERE TO MAKE IT."

"That's an excellent suggestion, Ms. Winthrop . . ." From Reflecting Men at Twice Their Natural Size by Sally Cline and Dale Spender. © 1987 by Sally Cline and Dale Spender. Reprinted by permission of Henry Holt and Co., Inc.

dence to the contrary, most organizations still assume that women are part of a traditional family in which the man is the primary earner and the woman tends to the home. Thus, childcare, eldercare, and other benefits women need are often not included in benefit packages. Even the benefits offered hourly and lower-level personnel assume that the beneficiary is a male supporting a family. Similarly, perks are usually tickets to sports events or memberships in golf clubs. The recent popularity of "cafeteria benefits," which allow employees to choose the kinds of benefits they want, suggests that companies are beginning to acknowledge women's different needs and preferences.

Another source of perceived devaluation on the organizational level is competency testing, which is related to the belief, usually subconscious, that women lack the skills needed to be leaders. Thus, if a woman competes with a man for a job or promotion and wins, her victory is attributed to special treatment or affirmative action mandates, not to her ability. If a man wins, he is assumed to be more competent than those with whom he competed.

A joke making the rounds among corporate women illustrates the competency-testing trap. A certain firm decided to hold its annual meeting on a beautiful fishing boat in the Bahamas. The company's vice president of corporate affairs was the only woman officer on the invitation list. The CEO wasn't sure she would attend, but she did. When the boat was about a mile from the dock, the woman vice president realized she had left her purse behind. The CEO told her they could not turn back. "That's okay," she said as she stepped off the deck and began to walk on the water toward shore. The CEO watched her and then turned to his male buddies and said, "See, I told you she couldn't swim!"

When women feel devalued on either the personal or the organizational level, they face a number of choices. Should they remain in an organization that doesn't appreciate them and hope to be the exception to the rule? Should they go to an organization where there is no differential treatment based on sex, even if it means a lateral or downward move? Should they leave corporate life altogether and become entrepreneurs? There is growing anecdotal evidence that women are leaving large traditional organizations to join smaller ones where "fitting in" is not required. Women also seem willing to step sideways or backwards even in difficult economic times if they believe their chances will improve in a more hospitable environment. And women are starting their own companies at twice the rate of men, suggesting that the entrepreneurial route, difficult as it may be, is preferable to feeling devalued.[21]

There is little doubt that many women change jobs, and sometimes even careers, out of a sense that their talents are not being fully utilized. In late 1991 Pacific Telesis, a large telecommunications company, surveyed women who had left the company. The key finding was that the majority reported having felt undervalued and underutilized while they worked there. The higher their level of education, the more underutilized these female ex-employees felt. Those with a high school education tended to feel valued. Of those with a bachelor's degree, 38 percent felt fully valued, and of those with a master's degree, only 10 percent. *None* of those with Ph.D.s felt fully valued or utilized.[22]

It isn't hard to find women whose stories substantiate this phenomenon. A former student of mine who had worked at a well-known CPA firm for seven years left because she felt that as a woman she had been denied the kind of assignments she would need to make partner, assignments her male colleagues received as a matter of course.[23] A partner in a major national law firm, who was a very successful litigator, watched the same thing happen in her field.

> While one of a handful of women litigation partners in my firm, I observed that women associates were often passed over in assignments for confrontational discovery work or settlement work, and relegated to the more academic and tamer work of motion preparation and argument. Women associates were often complimented for supportive assistance in helping a partner prepare a case for trial but were not encouraged to take risks or "take command" of a matter; even in litigation there was a tendency to caution women against becoming "too aggressive." The incomplete range of assignments and the encouragement of "helpmate" behavior made the women perfect associates—but too compliant, deferential, and inexperienced to be accepted as partners.[24]

Even women in family-owned businesses are not im-
mune to underutilization. Sharon Lundgren, an executive
and part-owner of Volcano Communications, told a *Wall
Street Journal* reporter that she had to go to court to purchase a majority interest in her family firm because her
parents and brother refused to sell it to her. She contended
that the dispute was related to her parents' sexist bias
against women running companies. She pointed to her
father's comments about keeping the company for her
brother (fourteen years her junior), and told the court she
was paid less than men in the company with fewer responsibilities than she had. Lundgren's is not the only case of
its kind. Many daughters have to fight for leadership positions in family-owned corporations, particularly when there
is a brother in the picture.[25]

These are not isolated stories. They reflect the subtle
and sometimes not so subtle marginalization that professional women experience. This is not to say that there are
not also men who are underutilized. Certainly there are.
However, when men are underutilized, it is usually for reasons other than their sex. Nor is it to say that all women
feel undervalued and underutilized, or that all men consciously or unconsciously devalue women's contributions.
But it is to say that a great many professional women feel
and believe that they are devalued because they are female.

This perception is not merely a figment of their imagi-
nations, as we'll see in the next chapter, which describes
five objective measures of female underutilization.

3

The Underutilization of Women

It is abundantly clear that professional women often feel devalued and underutilized. Since they're constantly having to prove their competence because they're different from the one best model, that isn't surprising. But what exactly does "underutilization" mean? What are its implications as organizations assess the connection between human resources and competitive advantage? Does being underutilized mean being unemployed, being underemployed, or being given responsibilities that don't match one's talents? Does it mean not being asked for advice, hitting a glass ceiling, or being underrepresented in managerial ranks? Does it mean not being able to advance because of gender-related performance criteria? Does it mean all of these? Such questions reveal the complexity of the underutilization concept as it relates to the one best model and the difference-as-deficiency mind-set.

To find out more about what is meant by underutilization, I surveyed male and female professionals in a wide variety of industries.[1] Regardless of their sex, professional title, or organizational setting, their replies were quite similar, with one exception. The president of an innovative mid-sized company that prides itself on an egalitarian corporate climate said that underutilization is a nonissue, a "corporate bullshit word." Since tapping into the potential of all employees is part of the culture of his firm, his response makes sense. The rest of the respondents *did* recognize the concept as an issue to which they have not paid sufficient attention. They said that underutilization means "not being challenged, motivated, or empowered," "not being used," "being assigned roles that don't fit one's skills," "not being required to perform tasks that take advantage of or build on one's education, experience, and ability."

There is little doubt that the term "underutilization" is perceived as related to untapped human resources. For purposes of this book, I define the underutilization of women as *the failure to use their existing or potential skills and talents primarily because they are women.*

The Measurement of Female Underutilization

The survey question "How would you *measure* underutilization?" elicited a much fuzzier message than the question asking for a definition. Replies to the measurement question were general and vague, indicating that the respondents found it hard to answer. Many made such suggestions as "get feedback," "ask people," "look at morale," or "examine job descriptions and results." However, these replies provide no "hook" for quantification. They offer no standards of measurement. One of the most concrete answers was: "The way to measure underutilization is to see if a person is in a position that could be performed by someone with less skill and education." This answer is useful but difficult to operationalize. What we learn from the survey is that it is difficult to measure underutilization and there is little agreement about how to do it.

Why has so little attention been paid to the measurement of underutilization? Is it because human resource utilization has not been a big issue until recently? Is it because we tend to measure only those things to which numbers are easily attached? For example, it is relatively easy to quantify hours worked, dollars generated, products manufactured, or clients seen. It's not so simple to measure work potential, feelings of being undervalued, or the leveraging of education and skills. Attaching numbers to these kinds of things is called behavioral accounting, a relatively new academic endeavor that is as yet untested. It is not surprising, therefore, that there has been a tendency to overlook behaviors and feelings that resist measurement.

Though it is difficult to measure the underutilization of women, that does not mean it cannot and should not be measured. There are some quantitative measures that indicate this phenomenon. While they are far from perfect, they are worthy of discussion. They are *unemployment and underemployment rates*, *underrepresentation percentages*, *occupational segregation figures*, and the *relative pay* of men and women. These quantitative measures provide a useful framework for analyzing the underutilization of women.

Unemployment and Underemployment as Measures of Underutilization

It is difficult to measure the underutilization of women using only unemployment rates or statistics on women who work part-time or are not working in their field of choice. But taken together, these figures provide a gauge of the number of women who are educated and capable of working in their fields and for a variety of reasons are not. These women constitute an underutilized resource.

The U.S. Department of Labor and the Census Bureau do not define or keep figures on the underutilization of women. The National Science Foundation, however, has developed an operational definition of an underutilization rate: "the proportion of those in the total labor force who are either unemployed but seeking employment, working part-time but seeking full-time jobs, or working involuntarily in a nonscientific job."[2] Such a definition, along with available measures of unemployment and underemployment, enables us to begin to understand the underutilization of women.

There are a number of sources of unemployment figures. However, the data is categorized in a way that makes it difficult to pinpoint unemployment figures for men and women by specific profession; much of it gives a general rather than a detailed picture. The *Statistical Abstract of the United States*, a major source of data, provides overall employment participation rates by gender. For example, it shows that in sales 8.2 percent of women versus 4.8 percent of men are unemployed; in protective services the unemployment rate for women is 6.1 percent, versus 4.5 percent for men; in the executive, administrative, and managerial specialties, 4 percent of women and 3.6 percent of men are unemployed.[3] And of people with master's degrees in engineering, the unemployment rate for women in 1989 was 3.2 percent, almost double the 1.7 percent figure for men.[4] These figures certainly suggest that there are gender differences, but more research is needed to nail down labor participation rates for men and women in particular professions. Unfortunately, the issue of underutilization has not yet become a category for those collecting data on unemployment.

Relative unemployment rates are at best a crude measure of the underutilization of women. Knowing that a larger percentage of men than women are employed doesn't explain the apparent discrepancy between the employment potential of women and their actual employment. Historically, however, men have been expected to pursue lifelong careers, while women have not; therefore, the numbers are not really a surprise.

Looking at underemployment along with unemployment provides a fuller picture of the reality of underutilization. Underemployment includes part-time work and involuntary work in a field outside one's specialty. As I said, women may work part-time or outside their fields for many reasons, but whatever the reason, these women represent a pool of talent that is not being utilized.

Susan Alberstein is one of many women who work part-time but would prefer to work full-time. She is married and has two children, ages seven and nine. They no longer need her undivided attention. Alberstein earned a Ph.D. in computer science before she got married in 1980. She desires a career as a professor. Her husband is a chemical engineer. He was offered just the kind of job he wanted with a company in a southern town where there would be few career opportunities for her. Since his salary would be more than she could make as a professor, and since good chemical engineering jobs are hard to find, they decided to accept the offer and move from the large city where they had been living to the small southern town. With no major college or university nearby, Alberstein couldn't find a teaching or research position. For a long time she was unemployed, intellectually unfulfilled, and economically underutilized. Eventually she became an underemployment statistic instead of an unemployment statistic when she began tutoring high school students part-time as a way to feel useful. She wonders whether her husband would have agreed to move if their roles had been reversed. She thinks not.

There are many Susan Albersteins in the United States. Having to move because of a husband's career needs is not unusual for professional women. Because of mobility issues, the fact that the male job usually pays more, and other circumstances beyond their control, women like Alberstein represent untapped human resources.

Full-time employment is defined as thirty-five hours a week or more. Part-time employees work one to thirty-four hours a week. In 1992 more than twenty million people in the United States were employed part-time, or 17.5 percent of all workers; women represented 66 percent of that 17.5 percent.[5] Like Susan Alberstein, some women work part-time because they can't find full-time employment where they live. Other women work part-time for family reasons. Still others work part-time because men get the full-time jobs women apply for.

Mary Jenks is a case in point. She received an M.B.A. in the mid-1980s and was happy as a financial analyst in a large Chicago bank. When the bank failed, she found herself pounding the pavement, like others with similar degrees and work experience. Unfortunately, at the same time she was handed her pink slip, Jenks was in the middle of a messy divorce. For six months she found herself job hunting and living off savings. As a result of the divorce, she became the primary support for her two small children. She wasn't worried, because she was sure she would find a job. To her dismay, she discovered that her male peers were receiving offers while she and her female colleagues received none. She didn't think much about the gender issue until she applied for a position in a small bank. She knew she was qualified. If anything, she felt she was overqualified.

A senior vice president of the bank interviewed her, and the interview went well. She was sure she would be hired. Several days later she received a call from a bank secretary asking that she meet with the senior vice president. Thinking he was offering her the position, she entered his office with a broad smile. When she saw his face, she knew something was wrong. He asked her to sit down, looked her in the eye, and said he felt obliged to tell her himself that she was not getting the job.

"Mary," he said, "I wanted to hire you because you would be an asset to our firm. However, after our interview I met with a young man who is also qualified. I have offered him the position. I want you to know why." She was curious, then shocked, as he continued. "In times like these I feel giving the job to you would mean denying it to a man who has a family to support." Jenks had never mentioned her family responsibilities to the vice president. She knew it was illegal for an employer to ask about marital issues. She wondered if the young man who was offered the job *had* a family to support, or if it was just assumed he did. The senior vice president had wrongly assumed she was married and working for "pin money."

Jenks could have filed a sexual discrimination complaint, but fortunately for the bank, she was impressed by the senior vice president's honesty and did nothing. However, she did begin to realize that being a woman can mean not being viewed as a breadwinner, and that when "breadwinning" is pitted against "pin money," men come out on top. Jenks continued to look for a full-time job, but she didn't find one. For financial reasons, she accepted a part-time job in hopes that it might lead to full-time employment and eventually put her back on her career track.

Women don't always work part-time because they can't find full-time jobs. Some women prefer part-time work, though increasingly so do men. As organizations downsize and entire industries restructure, there is a growing tendency to replace full-time employees with part-time contractors and consultants. This reduces overhead and allows for better cost control. Contingency work, temping, and consulting are familiar terms to male and female managers today.[6] However, putting in long hours is still considered a prime value in the labor market, and part-time work is not seen as a plus on a résumé.

Part-time work has other drawbacks. Part-time professionals usually do not receive benefits. It is assumed that spouses or partners have benefits. For men, who usually don't have spouses with good benefits, part-time work is especially troublesome. The same is true for single women. In other words, part-time work is desirable primarily in instances where one partner in a dual-career family is able to obtain good benefits from a full-time job.

As the figures indicate, women tend to work part-time more often than men. Since full-time jobs are associated with men, part-time work is devalued, and so are women and men who work part-time. This is changing as men begin to see the advantages of part-time work, especially if their wives have good benefits or if their benefit packages can be transferred. If more men begin to work part-time and shoulder more responsibility for raising their families, part-time work may be valued more. If more men find themselves unable to obtain full-time jobs, there may be a push for part-time benefit programs.

Another way to measure underemployment is to compare degrees granted in specific areas with labor participation rates in those areas. To put it differently, do men and women fully utilize their educations? Here some interesting gender differences emerge. For example, 38 percent of those who received M.D.'s in 1991 were women, but only 28 percent of working doctors in 1993 were women. In 1991, 43 percent of all law degrees went to women, but in 1993 only 29 percent of working lawyers were women. And in 1991, 15 percent of those who earned master's degrees in engineering were women, but in 1993 only 8 percent of working engineers were women.[7] We can generally assume that earning a degree, particularly in such professions as medicine, law, and engineering, prepares men and women for work in their area of specialization. If women are not employed in their professions, we can say that their talents are not being fully utilized.

Along with the relative unemployment data, the evidence that more women than men work part-time or do not work in their professions of choice or training supports the contention that the talents of these women are not being fully tapped.

Underrepresentation as a Measure of Underutilization

The underrepresentation of women in institutional positions of power is no secret. Studies by the nonprofit Catalyst, the

Korn/Ferry executive search firm, and the U.S. Department of Labor continue to show that although women are moving from lower to middle management, they remain scarce in top leadership positions.[8] It is this underrepresentation of women at the top that seems to be a never-ending problem.

As mentioned previously, the glass ceiling metaphor suggests that women can see where they want to go but bump their heads as they try to get there. The percentage of women in executive jobs (those with major budget and line responsibility) has not changed much over the past fifteen years, yet an increasingly large number of professional women have received degrees in medicine, law, accountancy, education, finance, and to a lesser extent computer science and engineering. Many studies calculate the number of female senior managers in the major U.S. firms at less than 5 percent.[9]

In large law firms the percentage of women partners remains far below the percentage of male partners when education and experience are held constant. The same is true for large CPA firms.[10] In 1994 the percentage of female partners at the Big Six accounting firms was 5.3, not much of an improvement over the 4.1 percent reported five years earlier.[11] In large universities, and particularly schools of business, the story is no different. Most chancellors, presidents, and deans are male. A 1992 *Business Week* article notes that "only 8% of the tenured faculty at *Business Week*'s top 20 business schools are women . . . and at several prominent B-schools, including those at Dartmouth College and Washington University, not one woman is tenured."[12] An article in the *New York Times* tells the same story for medical schools, where female academic physicians are less likely to be promoted and given administrative positions.[13]

Only one woman CEO shows up on the list in the Fortune 500, although the number of top women executives in small and medium firms is probably larger.[14] Women who become officers of major companies are more likely than not to be in staff rather than line positions, and although this is changing, it is changing slowly. Even in female-dominated occupations, men continue to sit in most of the seats in the executive suite. The same pattern appears on boards of directors. In 1994 only 6.2 percent of the seats on Fortune 500 and Service 500 company boards were held by women. Very few corporate boards have more than one woman.[15]

One of the problems with quantifying the underrepresentation of women is that there is no widely accepted definition of middle or upper managers, or of what constitutes significant representation. The Census Bureau uses a definition that lumps office managers together with CEOs. Academics use categories not always comparable to the census definition. Corporations sometimes use a broad definition to show that they have a "good" record with women. For these reasons, the underrepresentation measure is troublesome. However, it is safe to say that women are currently underrepresented in top executive positions in all occupations and industries and in government. Surgery, considered the premier medical specialty, remains male-dominated.[16] Litigation, one of the most respected areas of law, is considered a male domain.[17] Symphony conductors and art museum directors are predominantly male, as are chancellors and presidents of educational institutions. Most retailing, fashion, and cosmetics firms are led by men. Ironically, even executive chefs are mostly male, although women are often told that the kitchen is their proper place.

Concerned with the underrepresentation issue, the U.S. Merit Systems Protection Board completed a study of women in government white-collar jobs in late 1992. The findings further confirm the glass ceiling problem and the underutilization of women.

... barriers do exist that have resulted in women, overall, being promoted less often ... than men with comparable education and experience. Women are promoted at a lower rate than men in grade levels and occupations that are important gateways to advancement. The women we surveyed express the same level of commitment to their jobs and careers as men, and women receive the same or better performance ratings as men, but their potential for advancement is often underestimated by managers using criteria which they traditionally have seen as a way to measure job commitment and advancement potential.[18]

Not only are women underrepresented in executive suites, ivory towers, and the U.S. Congress, they are also underrepresented on the speaker's dais at most professional meetings. Mary E. Clutter, assistant director for biological sciences at the National Science Foundation, tells the story of how she turned down a request for funds for an important research conference because no women were invited to speak. A prominent male scientist on the conference committee asked Clutter to reverse her decision. Since the work of women scientists was being presented, he wondered why she was upset that only men were making the presentations.[19] The answer would be obvious to most women. Representation, whether on corporate boards or conference programs, has much to do with credibility and legitimacy. A conference where only men give talks or present research findings reinforces the notion that women are somehow deficient by definition. To paraphrase an old E. F. Hutton ad, some believe that when women talk, no one listens.

Occupational Segregation as a Measure of Underutilization

If women are underrepresented in positions of power in American institutions, they are also found primarily in professions and occupations that have low status and low pay. "Men and women in the labor force are not distributed equally across occupations. This inequality in distribution is termed occupational segregation: the labor market segregates women disproportionately into certain occupations,

"I'M SO PROUD TO BE PART OF A PROFESSION THAT HAS NEVER DISCRIMINATED AGAINST WOMEN."

"I'm so proud to be part of a profession . . ." © 1995 by Sidney Harris.

men into others," writes Professor Myra Strober of Stanford University, an authority on occupational segregation.[20] In the United States, secretarial work, nursing, education, social work, and retail are female-dominated professions. Engineering, medicine, construction, manufacturing, public safety, and forestry are male-dominated occupations. There are historical reasons for this, yet while women today are increasingly entering male-dominated professions like business, medicine, and engineering, men are not entering female-dominated professions in anywhere near similar numbers. Strober suggests that "occupational segregation inhibits men and women from choosing occupations in accordance with their talents and tastes and may thereby decrease the overall efficiency and productivity of the economy and the well-being of those whose aspirations are restricted."[21]

Dr. Frances Conley, professor of neurosurgery at the Stanford University Medical School, notes that career counselors are directing more and more women into primary care medicine while men continue to choose elite medical specialties, which is further segregating the medical profession. This phenomenon is beginning to be seen throughout the world. Conley predicts that the result will be a two-tier system of medicine where primary care physicians are predominantly women with low status and low pay, and specialists are predominantly men with high status and high pay.[22]

The experience of Debbie Hoffman illustrates how occupational segregation contributes to the underutilization of women. As director of surgical nursing at Good Samaritan, a large Los Angeles hospital, Hoffman was responsible for the operating room twenty-four hours a day. In this capacity she was a professional manager rather than a nurse. Yet she knew she was viewed as a nurse, not a manager, even though she was accountable to the hospital director. As Hoffman discovered, women in managerial positions in nursing are rarely seen as credible, even when they receive advanced degrees in management and have management skills the doctors lack.

Hoffman, a single parent of two, realized that her managerial talents were not being fully utilized in her position as director of nursing. She decided to leave her job in search of a career where her talents would be valued. After enrolling in finance and budgeting courses at a local college in order to build on her nursing knowledge and managerial experience, she switched from nursing to business. Today she is an account executive with a health care manufacturer. Her sales record exceeds that of many of her male peers, and she is treated with great respect by physicians who rely on her advice. The same physicians who patron ized her when she managed their operating rooms now treat her more like a colleague. They see her as a technical sales rep, not a nurse.

Women like Debbie Hoffman are leaving nursing and nursing management in large numbers because they are undervalued and unable to make the most of their talents. As long as women have less credibility or lower status merely because they are in female-dominated occupations and professions, this trend will continue.

Nursing is an obvious example of occupational segregation based on sex. Similarly, engineering is a sex-segregated occupation dominated by men. When a woman moves into management in an engineering or manufacturing firm, she makes headlines in the business sections of all the major newspapers. Executives like Sandra Kurtzig, CEO of ASK Computer, Audrey Maclean, CEO of NET, June Rokoff, senior vice president of Lotus Development, and Debi Coleman, formerly with Apple Computer and currently CEO of Merix Corporation, prove that women can make it to the top in traditional male occupations. But because there are so few women in technical fields, successful women are considered "exceptional." Why is it that when women study math, engineering, and science, they do as well as men on standardized tests such as the SAT but don't become engineers and scientists?[23]

Pay Inequity as a Measure of Underutilization

If women are in sex-segregated occupations, if they are underrepresented in positions of authority, and if they are underemployed, it follows that they are probably underpaid as well. Pay inequity is another objective measure that can be linked to underutilization, and perhaps the most obvious, since it is assumed that pay reflects performance. The concept of meritocracy is alive and well in America because everyone likes to think performance rewards are based on merit. If they were, women who are as educated, experienced, and skilled as men would receive similar pay, but they don't. While the pay gap is closing, it is closing slowly, and more so in some occupations and industries than in others.

Considering overall earnings of all full-time employees, women in 1992 earned 25 percent less than men. This aggregate figure masks differences in various fields. Women engineers in 1989 earned 86 percent of what male engineers earned. Women nurses earned 11 percent less than male nurses doing the same jobs (further evidence that occupational segregation does not mean professional equality for women). More than half of all trained psychologists are women, yet they earn 17 percent less than their male colleagues.[24] Female physicians in private practice earn 34 percent less than their male colleagues.[25] Female lawyers make 75 cents for every dollar earned by male lawyers. Female financial managers make 59 cents for every dollar made by male peers.[26] Corporate women consistently earn less than comparable males. Pay in the corporate world is a perfect example of the overvaluing of male CEOs and the undervaluing of women. When it comes to salaries and bonuses, in 1993 the highest-paid corporate executive below the level of CEO was a woman, Turi Josefsen, executive vice president of U.S. Surgical Corporation, who earned $23.6 million. However, she was the exception.[27]

Knowing that pay inequity exists does not tell us why it exists. One major contributing factor is the traditional concept of the man as breadwinner, which also accounts in part for female unemployment, underemployment, and underrepresentedness, and is not unrelated to occupational segregation. Since men have generally brought home the primary household income in the past, women are often felt to be working for reasons other than necessity. This may explain why men and women who do the same job are not always paid the same salary. As Mary Jenks discovered, there is still a sense that a woman's income is secondary to her husband's. Yet in many households today women are the primary or the only breadwinners.

Another explanation for pay inequity is the belief that women lack good negotiation skills and don't ask for the same starting salaries or raises as men do. There is some support for this idea. Because women often expect to be treated fairly, they don't realize they need to think about what a fair wage is. I frequently hear stories from women who tell me that the salary attached to their former positions went up when they were replaced by men. They attribute this to the fact that men request more and bargain more than women. It has also been suggested that professional women think in terms of "relative deprivation," which means they feel they are so much better off than other women that they should be happy with what they get.[28]

One other widely held belief is that women drop in and out of the labor force to have children, so that they can't possibly have as much work experience as men. Having children is often seen as a signal to an employer that a woman may not stay, so less investment in her is justified. Yet even when work experience and education are held constant, women often earn less than male counterparts.[29]

Although more a tool for examining pay inequity than an explanation, the concept of comparable worth sheds light on the pay differential between women and men. Whatever the reason, female occupations command lower pay than male occupations. For example, truck drivers make more money than nurses, and janitors often make as much as teachers. The theory of comparable worth, which was popular in the 1970s, attempts to address the pay inequity problem by assigning values to occupations based on experience, skill level, education, and level of responsibility required. Using this method, it can be shown that the qualifications needed to be a nurse are considerably greater than those needed by a truck driver. Thus, it is possible to establish the comparable worth of each job category.[30]

Most studies show that women are paid less than men in most occupations and professions.[31] A study I conducted of executive men and women suggested some exceptions to that rule. I found that in organizations that value women there is no pay inequity.[32] Like the other measures of underutilization, pay inequity may be related to the larger organizational culture. It appears that when women are genuinely valued, they are paid the same as men.

The Mismeasure of Woman

For some time, economists have been interested in women's participation in the workforce, although they have only recently begun to investigate why women hit a glass ceiling. Most economists explain labor participation differences, occupational choices, and pay inequity in terms of market forces. They talk about male-female differences in the context of what men and women each bring to the market.

Many economists contend that women don't make the same investment in their careers as men—that is, they don't have as many degrees, they don't work as hard, or they are not as committed.[33] On this view, the differential career patterns and rewards associated with men and women are the market's response to their different investments. However, some economic studies suggest that gender discrimination interferes with the market system. Controlling for "investment factors" such as education and experience, these studies show that men are promoted faster and earn larger incomes than women across a wide range of professions and industries.[34]

Some economists use "family power theory" to explain how the market system works to disadvantage women.[35] They say that women sacrifice their careers to further those of their partners, the assumption being that men hold the most powerful positions in families. In accommodating their husbands' careers, women are often forced to leave good jobs of their own. They may end up working part-time in order to play the role of executive wife. They may put off obtaining a graduate degree because it interferes with their partner's job advancement. Or they may abandon the idea of a career altogether. Family power theorists have a point. As we saw, the assumption that the man is the primary breadwinner was certainly at work in the cases of Susan Alberstein and Mary Jenks.

Until recently, career development has been studied in a generic way, without regard to gender differences.[36] Now, however, women's career development has emerged as a separate topic. For example, Helen Astin's career development theory suggests that men and women have similar basic work motivations but that they make different career choices because their early socialization experiences and the opportunities presented to them differ. Astin notes that women are often not able to make clear-cut career choices. Unlike men, they must factor in constraints placed upon them by the attitudes of a spouse, family responsibilities, economic concerns, etc. Such outside factors have not usually been included in the study of women's career choices.[37]

In his provocative book *Women's Quest for Economic Equality*, Professor Victor Fuchs of Stanford University says that the economic disparity between men and women stems from the conflict between work and family rather than from career investment patterns. He believes that this conflict is stronger for women than for men, and will remain so for the foreseeable future. For Fuchs, the key to female underutilization is the cost to women of combining work and family, a cost not borne equally by men.[38]

Fuchs is an economist and makes his argument in cost-benefit terms. From their perspective as psychologists, Veronica F. Nieva and Barbara A. Gutek also make the case that as long as women shoulder the major responsibility for home and family, their career choices will continue to differ from those of men and sexual discrimination in the workplace will not disappear.[39] Arlie Hochschild, in *The Second Shift*, supports this view and provides convincing evidence that career women, unlike men, work a second shift at home because household tasks remain a female chore.

"Balancing a job and a family . . ." "The Working Woman Book-or-How to Be Everything to Everyone" by Barbara and Jim Dale. © 1985 by Barbara and Jim Dale.

Thus, women are unable to take advantage of the same career opportunities as men.[40] Lotte Bailyn, in *Breaking the Mold,* contends that home and work cannot be seen as separate domains if women are to have the same opportunities as men. As she writes, "The key question is whether one can devise organizational processes that deal simultaneously with productivity and with family or other personal concerns, and do not depend for their success on highly differentiated gender roles."[41] Bailyn pushes for a rethinking of the concept of work and how it is evaluated. She persuasively argues that technological advances and new workplace structures make the integration of work and family possible and economically beneficial.

The common thread that runs through most recent career development theory is that we can no longer blame the victims or rely on the female deficiency thesis to explain the underutilization of women. Training women to act like men is no longer fashionable. No longer can employers assume that because a woman is raising children, she will want to be placed on a "mommy track" that gives her more time off but slows her career advancement.[42] There is a new awareness that the barriers women face in the workplace probably have more to do with the one best model than with their aptitudes and preferences.

Among those who don't share this new awareness are various economists who believe that women purposely choose low-paying careers.[43] That is, women decide to be teachers, nurses, and social workers, instead of truck drivers or plumbers, knowing full well the implications of their choices. If women want bigger incomes, say these economists, they should forget about comparable worth and pursue careers in occupations that pay better. However, this brand of choice theory does not explain why plumbing and trucking, traditionally male occupations requiring less education than teaching and nursing, pay more. Nor does it explain why male nurses advance faster than female nurses, all other things being equal, or why the supply-and-demand thesis doesn't account for the pay disparity. But it satisfies those who believe that the market determines what's valued and what isn't. If women are underutilized, according to these economists, it's because they don't pay attention to market forces. The market, they insist, ensures equity. But does it?

It is true that market forces cannot be ignored in the attempt to understand why women are underutilized. But economic theories by themselves don't give us sufficient answers because they posit "ideal" market forces and perfect information, neither of which exists. There is no perfect market, and there is no perfect economic explanation for the underutilization of women.

When I speak to business audiences and ask why they think women are underutilized, they often offer explanations based on theories from a wide variety of disciplines. For instance, they suggest that women hit the glass ceiling because of sex differences rooted in female biology or in the way women are socialized. However, it frequently turns out that what they mean is that women don't measure up to the one best male model. They marshal biological or sociological theories to suggest that women don't have the "right stuff," but they neglect to mention, or perhaps aren't even aware, that having the right stuff means meeting the male standards by which women are measured.

In and of themselves, biological and sociological theories offer little guidance in matters of gender. The debate over the relative importance of heredity and environment in determining gender differences is never-ending and probably unresolvable. For that reason I agree with those who say we should be less concerned about the nature/nurture causality of gender differences and more concerned about parity between men and women.[44] In other words, we should concentrate on appreciating gender differences rather than arguing about their origins.

In the context of underutilization, it really doesn't matter whether gender differences are a product of nature or nurture. In either case, the problem is not the differences but the one-best-model mind-set. In either case, the challenge is to make sure that we *value* difference rather than denigrate it, and that standards of excellence recognize both male and female attributes. Indeed, the real importance of the nature/nurture debate may be to highlight the fact that standards of measurement need to be inclusive rather than exclusive.[45]

In *The Mismeasure of Woman*, Carol Tavris suggests that if workplace performance standards were female, it would be men who were seen as different and therefore deficient.[46] Tavris is not proposing that the one best male model be replaced by a one best female model. Rather, her point is that differences between the sexes must be analyzed nonpejoratively and that standards must be based on competence, not gender. Currently, gender plays too large a role in performance assessments and creates too many obstacles to the full utilization of women. What accounts for this, I think, is sexual static.

4

Sexual Static

Whatever their fundamental origin, gender differences give rise to a subtle phenomenon seldom taken into account in discussions of women in the workplace. I call this phenomenon "sexual static."[1]

Sexual static is like snow on the television set or noise on the radio—it causes interference with messages being communicated. In the workplace, messages sent between men and women are difficult to understand because of sexual static in the air. Both men and women experience sexual static. It causes frustration for women and discomfort for men. Women are frustrated because they feel the static could be minimized if men understood gender differences. Men just want the static to go away. They feel working with women means walking on eggshells, and although they're not sure what causes the static, they know it's associated with the presence of women. For this reason, men subconsciously find excuses for excluding women from the executive suite. As the *Wall Street Journal* report on the glass ceiling put it, "The biggest obstacle women face is also the most intangible; men at the top feel uncomfortable beside them."[2]

It's difficult to measure sexual static, because men don't like to admit they're confused or uncomfortable working with women, and even if they did, discomfort is very subjective. Nor do women want to admit they're the cause of male discomfort. But since sexual static leads to the underutilization of women, it cannot be ignored. In the next chapter men's feelings and their reaction to sexual static will be fully explored. However, first it is necessary to understand the sources of sexual static and its relationship to the underutilization of women. Apart from office romance and sexual harassment—obvious sources of sexual static that are discussed only in passing since so much has been written about them and their impact on work interactions[3]— these sources can be categorized as follows: (1) *role confusion,* or confusion about the changing roles of men and women at work; (2) *garbled communication,* or differences in the way men and women communicate; and (3) *culture clash,* or the conflict between male and female cultural values. Individually and collectively, these generate sexual static.

Role Confusion

Most of us grew up with specific expectations about how we were supposed to behave as girls and boys, women and men. This socialization process begins at birth, but as Jean Lipman-Blumen says, "Pink and blue blankets are only the symbolic tip of the socialization iceberg."[4]

It is no secret that parents, doctors, nurses, and others who interact with newborns treat girl babies and boy babies differently. In an experiment recounted by Lipman-Blumen, nurses were handed male newborns wrapped in pink blankets and female newborns wrapped in blue blankets. In almost all cases, the nurses handled the infants in the blue blankets, assumed to be boys, much less carefully than those in the pink blankets, assumed to be girls.[5] The differential treatment continues as babies grow. Parents buy dolls for girls and cars for boys. Boys are allowed to be boisterous and noisy. Girls are expected to be quiet and cooperative. Boys pick up sticks that soon become guns. Girls pick up sticks that become magic wands. No one knows if heredity or environment accounts for these differences. Sociologists point to environmental factors, but mothers who have tried to raise children in a nonsexist way might be tempted to vote for heredity.

The socialization of males and females takes place both within and outside the home. As children grow up, they see that nurses are women and doctors are men, teachers are women and principals are men, secretaries are women and CEO's are men, and so on. Thus, sex role expectations are reinforced by everyday experience. Girls learn that their role in life is to provide service and support, and boys learn that their role in life is to command and control.[6] It should therefore be no surprise that when girls and boys become adults and enter the workforce, they experience "sex role spillover."[7] That is, the sex role expectations of early childhood spill over into the work environment, where men are clearly expected to be in control and women are clearly expected to provide service and support. This explains why the first wave of women executives tended to be in staff positions—in human resources, public relations, and legal departments, for example—rather than line positions. A staff position is consistent with female role expectations. Men feel comfortable with women managers in support functions.

Today these expectations have changed, and there is a great deal of role confusion. Men and women are constantly bombarded with a blurring of role expectations. On the one hand, they hear that men and women alike are free to make any career choice they wish; on the other hand, they hear that traditional values need to be reinstated and that women should stay at home because families are suffering from the absence of mothers.

A friend of mine owns a large mergers and acquisitions firm that buys and sells companies. She was on her way from Los Angeles to New York for a business meeting when her plane was delayed. While she was waiting in an airport bar, a man approached her. "Hello, would you like a little company?" he asked. "Sure" she said. "Do you have one for sale?" She was thinking business, he was thinking female. This sort of misunderstanding is common today, now that women are in professions and managerial positions that have historically been all male. It's no wonder men are confused.

For many years I have been collecting data from professional men and women about their perceptions of gender differences. As I visit organizations across the country, I ask people to list the words that first come to mind when they hear the word "leader." The words that appear most often are these.

Words Associated with "Leader"

- Strong
- Rational
- Independent
- Linear thinker
- Aggressive
- Competitive

When I ask women to list the words that come to mind when they hear the word "male," these are the words they mention.

Words Women Associate with "Male"

- Strong
- In control/domineering
- Husband/father/brother
- Macho
- Power
- Rational

70

When I give talks to male and female managers, I show these responses on a slide. A woman attending one talk raised her hand and said she didn't think men were rational. "If they were," she said, "they would ride horses side-saddle!" The women in the audience laughed. But however rationality or any other attribute is defined, when we look at the two lists of free associations, it is obvious that in general the attributes associated with leaders are similar to the attributes associated with men. This simple exercise shows why women are not seen in terms of leadership potential: they don't exhibit male attributes.

When I ask men to list the words that come to mind when they hear the word "woman," it's clear they aren't thinking of leaders. The words they most often list are these.

Words Men Associate with "Female"

- Sex
- Mother/wife
- Beauty
- Soft/curves
- Sensitive

"Sex" is usually the first or second word on the list when men are asked to think about women. It is usually sixth or seventh on the list when women are asked to think about men. This is not to say that women don't enjoy sex but that sex is not the first thing they think about when they think about men. The importance of this word-association exercise is that it reveals men's tendency to view women in terms of their sexuality rather than in terms of their leadership potential. Since words structure thought, the lists provide a clue to a source of sexual static for men when they interact with women at work: they view them initially in a sexual rather than a work context.

Notice that none of the words men use to describe women are similar to the words associated with leaders. This suggests why men are so confused about whether women can lead. If men see women in terms of their sexuality, or as they see their wives and mothers, then they are forced to change gears when they encounter women as peers, competitors, or leaders. This sense of having to shift gears is a major source of sexual static for men. (In my talks I do not ask women to list the attributes they associate with women, although the responses would be interesting. But because it is men who are in a position to recruit and promote women, I focus on male perceptions of women as key to understanding the underutilization issue.)

When I ask professional women what they would like men at work to change, this is what they say.

What Women Want Men to Change

- Be honest about the fact that they are uncomfortable working with women.
- Stop being so patronizing.
- Take women seriously and treat us like professionals.
- Stop sexist remarks and jokes.

These responses suggest that women know how confused men feel about changing female roles, and that they want men to talk about their discomfort. Women hope that in the process of talking about their own feelings, men will begin to understand why women feel devalued.

When I ask men what they would like women at work to change, these are their responses.

What Men Want Women to Change

- Stop being so defensive.
- Don't try to be masculine.
- Be more assertive.
- Don't be so emotional.
- Be more self-confident.

This list says it all. It shows sex role spillover in action. It reveals the confusion men experience in working with professional women. The responses are full of contradictions, what psychologists call "cognitive dissonance,"[8] or conflicting thoughts. Men want women to act like men—that is, be more confident, unemotional, and assertive—but at the same time they want them to be feminine. They want women to stop being defensive, yet they make them feel defensive by treating them as sex objects. The list seems to echo Henry Higgins in *My Fair Lady*, who asked, "Why can't a woman be more like a man?" at the same time that he was thinking "Vive la difference!"

A similar dynamic is at work in the different leadership styles men and women prefer, as we can see if we look again at the behaviors associated with each.

Command-and-Control Leadership Style

- Top-down decision making
- Use of structural power
- Focus on self-interest of followers
- Control by reward for specific tasks
- Stress on individual contribution
- Emphasis on "rational" decision making

Interactive Leadership Style

- Shared decision making
- Use of personal power
- Focus on achievement of organizational goals
- Control by generating empowerment
- Stress on shared power and information
- Emphasis on nontraditional forms of decision making

Like the word lists, these lists reflect very different ways of looking at the world. It's not only that men prefer the command-and-control style but that it *defines* leadership for them. Thus, when men encounter women who use the interactive leadership style, they may have difficulty recognizing them as leaders at all. Conversely, when they encounter women leaders who have adopted the command-and-control style, they may have difficulty relating to them as women. I suspect that this role confusion is exacerbated for men by the new interest in the interactive leadership style in many organizations. The possibility that interactive leadership may sometimes be more effective than command-and-control leadership in today's organizational environment creates sexual static for men because it makes them realize that their style may not be the only one that works.

The role confusion illustrated by the lists also shows up in work-related social gatherings in which it is still assumed that the men are the invitees and the women are their spouses. Both women and men tell stories of how confusing this can be. In the case of a high-ranking male GOP official at a White House gathering in 1992, it turned out to be a disaster. Kathryn Thompson, CEO of a major development company in California, made a $100,000 contribution to George Bush's presidential campaign and thus became a member of what was called Team 100. She and the other Team 100 members were invited to a party in their honor. Of the twelve attendees she was the only woman present. The GOP official approached her and said, "And little lady, to whom do you belong?" After controlling her anger, she looked him in the eye and said, "I used to belong to Team 100!"

Garbled Communication

It's not surprising that Deborah Tannen's *You Just Don't Understand* topped the best-seller lists for a number of years.[9] Its popularity attests to the fact that garbled communication between men and women is common. Tannen says that men and women live in different worlds; thus, conversation between them is like cross-cultural communication. John Gray believes that it's not just a matter of different worlds but different planets; hence the title of his best-seller, *Men Are from Mars, Women Are from Venus.*[10] Both authors believe that women speak and hear a language of connection and intimacy, and men speak and hear a language of status and independence. Men communicate to obtain information, establish their status, and show independence. Women communicate to create relationships, encourage interaction, and exchange feelings. This difference creates sexual static.

Just as Tannen's book alerts men and women to their own respective communication styles, the movie *Thelma and Louise* shows how men and women selectively perceive

SINGLE SLICES   by Peter Kohlsaat

"You know . . . men and women speak . . ." © 1993, Los Angeles Times Syndicate. Reprinted with permission.

messages communicated to them. I have asked many mixed audiences to talk about the message *Thelma and Louise* conveys. Almost always, men describe the movie as a female *Sundance Kid*. They talk about what the gun-toting women did in the movie—got angry, swore, frequented bars, left their mates. Women, on the other hand, talk about how Thelma and Louise felt, how they were controlled by the men in their lives and would rather be dead than oppressed. Both messages are communicated. However, the fact that men and women interpret the movie so differently says something about how men and women think and view the world.

Men talk about what they do. Women talk about how they feel. This gender difference is important because men think that talking about feelings at work is unprofessional but talking about doing is okay. Men are confused and uncomfortable listening to women at work. Women don't understand why men are so hesitant to talk about feelings, and men don't understand why women spend so much time talking about feelings. The point is that neither talking about feelings nor talking about doing is necessarily related to work. Nonetheless, women's tendency to talk about personal feelings is a source of irritation to men, and that frustrates women, who don't see why it's not acceptable.

Men and women not only communicate about different things but their manner of communicating differs. Men tend to speak declaratively, as in "I want the report by Friday." Women are likely to ask, "Will the report be done by Friday?" The declarative statement seems more leaderlike because it is consistent with the traditional command-and-control leadership style.

In addition to being more declarative than women, men also tend to express themselves in fewer words. Women frequently leave their sentences dangling. They surround their statements with "I'm not sure, but . . ." or "You may not agree, but . . ." Sometimes this is because of low self-esteem, but often it is because women tend to think while they speak. Thus, what seems to men like female babbling or excessive verbiage is normal talk to women. Men's irritation with this stylistic difference comes across in comments like "Get to the point," "Spit it out," or "What are you trying to say?" It's clear that the way women tend to talk is another source of sexual static for men.

Men and women also seem to differ in the way they think, an idea that captured the public's fancy some years ago when there was a spate of books and articles about "right-brained" (female) versus "left-brained" (male) cognition.[11] Dr. Joe E. Bogen, a renowned neurosurgeon who has spent his life studying the brain, says, "It is clear that there are, on average, gender differences in the brain."[12] The early work of Jerre Levy and the work of Professor Doreen Kimura at the University of Western Ontario supports Bogen's view. "It would be amazing if men's and women's brains were not different, given the gross morphological and often striking behavioral differences between men and women which are not restricted to their different roles in parenting and reproductive behavior," Kimura writes.[13] The discovery by Professor Christine de Lacoste-Utamsing that the corpus callosum—a mass of nerve fibers that connect the brain hemispheres—is larger in women than in men suggests that women may process information differently because there is more communication between the right and left halves of the brain.[14]

The cognitive differences most often identified by researchers are the "better" performance of men on certain spatial tasks and in mathematical reasoning, and the "better" performance of women on verbal fluency tasks and tests of perceptual speed.[15] These differences are thought to be associated with the way the brain is organized. Notice that the word "better" is used to characterize the differences. It is this that causes sparks, ignites debate, and provides fuel for the one-best-model assumption, since the mental processes women are "better" at are often devalued outside the laboratory.

Women seem to order the information housed in their brains in a mysterious way and to arrive at answers by putting the information together in a holistic fashion. This is what is meant by "women's intuition." The word "scatterbrained," also associated with women, describes a way of thinking in which there is no apparent cohesive organization of data. It suggests that information is floating around in disconnected pieces and that the thought process is not linear or logical. Because processing information in a linear manner has been labeled "rational" and "logical," the judgments of women who think intuitively are often seen as untrustworthy. As long as the linear processing of information is considered "better," women who communicate in a nonlinear fashion are apt to be misunderstood and devalued.

Garbled communication can also be related to the way in which words are used. For example, many men can't understand why their wives, but not their female colleagues, like to be called girls. It doesn't occur to men that professional women don't want to be treated like wives. Nor do they realize why this is so. The word "girl" is defined in the dictionary as "a young person" or "a female servant or employee." "Girl" connotes youth, which women like, but it also implies low status. "Lady" is another troublesome word for some women. The word has many meanings, most of them having to do with good breeding, propriety, domestic management, or "receiving the homage or devotion of a knight or lover." That is, "lady" connotes a woman of social position. Like "girl," it is value-laden. The word "woman," however, simply describes an adult human being, and is an analog for the word "man." That is why most professional women prefer to be called women.

Granted, not all women are equally concerned about the words used to address or describe them. Nevertheless, words communicate status and tell a great deal about the way people think. While word usage may seem inconsequential to men, it is often a source of distress for women. When the issue is raised, men frequently say to women, "Why do you have a chip on your shoulder?" or "You're being oversensitive." In reality women are only trying to make communication gender-neutral and to reduce the amount of garbled communication.

Touching is another area fraught with potential misunderstandings. Touching is not only a way of showing affection, it is also a way of exercising power. People "touch down," they don't "touch up." People in positions of power tend to touch subordinates, but subordinates generally don't touch bosses. Since men have historically been the bosses and women the subordinates, women have accepted touching as part of their jobs. Until recently, most women didn't complain much about being touched, though today many women speak up when touched in ways they consider inappropriate. They have also discovered the need to be careful about touching male colleagues, so that their own behavior will not be viewed as inappropriate. Men worry much more today that touching in the wrong place, at the wrong time, or in the wrong way will be construed as sexual harassment. They find themselves being very careful about touching. Since individuals react to touching differently, it is difficult to develop workplace guidelines for touching behavior. For this reason, touching remains a major source of garbled communication.

Men and women communicate in nonverbal ways other than touching. The way they look, sit, walk, and carry themselves sends messages. In general women tend to be more sensitive to body language than men because as organizational outsiders they use nonverbal cues as a survival tool.[16] Being insiders, men don't need to pay attention to body language because they know the rules. Men and women don't interpret body language in the same way. A man may give a female colleague the familiar "up and down look" and think he's paying her a compliment, whereas the woman may see it as an insult. She may feel she is being viewed as a sex object rather than a professional peer. Thus, nonverbal communication can also become garbled and contribute to sexual static.

Culture Clash

The sexual static generated by the combination of role confusion and garbled communication would seem to be reason enough for men to feel confused and uncomfortable
working with women. Yet there is still another source of
sexual static: culture clash.

What is meant by this term? First, what is meant by
the word "culture"? It has been defined in a variety of ways.
For our purposes, it is "a system of shared meaning."[17] We
have already seen that because of their different experiences
men and women have different systems of shared knowledge and meaning. In other words, then, they live in different cultures, as John Gray and Deborah Tannen argue. This
is not to say that men and women don't have a common
culture based on experiences they share as human beings.
Rather, in addition to their common culture, men and
women have unique cultural characteristics by virtue of
their sex. This is no secret. Boys and girls play different
kinds of games, read different kinds of books, shoulder
different kinds of family responsibilities, and talk about
different kinds of things. So do men and women. When
male and female cultures come into conflict, culture clash
occurs.

The definition of culture as a system of shared meaning
helps explain the power of men in the workplace, where the
dominant culture is male. Few would disagree that men
hold most positions of authority in American institutions.
Because of their shared experiences as men, they have an
advantage when it comes to learning the rules of the organizational game and playing by them. That's because the
rules are based on the male experience. Given the perva-
siveness of the assimilation model, those in subcultures—
e.g., women and people of color—have to learn the rules of
the dominant culture in order to succeed.[18] Granted, women
and men may share the belief that employees should be re-

warded on performance, that honesty is the best policy, that "quality is job one," that it's important to pay attention to customers or constituents, and so on. But men and women would probably differ on how to reward performance, what is meant by honesty, what is meant by quality, and even what constitutes a customer. Because male culture is the dominant culture of the workplace, it is men's shared meanings that prevail.

Historically, there have been so few women in upper or even upper middle management that there was little questioning of the dominant culture. It was assumed that the behaviors and attitudes of those in the dominant group should be emulated. However, in the late 1970s and 1980s, when women began to join the workforce in large numbers looking for careers, not jobs, they found themselves at a disadvantage because they did not share the dominant culture. They started asking questions, and the clash of cultures began. Their questions were prompted by their inability or unwillingness to assimilate to the one best model. They wondered why working long hours, as men could do because they had wives at home, was better than working shorter hours, as women wanted to do, if the same amount of work was accomplished. They wondered why companies offered paid time off for drug and alcohol rehabilitation but not for parental leave. They wondered why golf or drinking after work was considered an important part of bringing in business but women's social activities were not. They wondered why life insurance for a spouse was considered a major benefit when many women were single or had spouses with their own insurance.

Today, women continue to question some of the basic assumptions implicit in the dominant culture. They question the command-and-control leadership style, the hiding of emotions, the criteria used to measure performance, and the importance of golf. They are not asking that the dominant male culture be replaced but that it be expanded in a way that values the female culture. Women are asking that the dominant culture be *inclusive* rather than *exclusive*. They want performance criteria that reflect the worth of the female way of doing things, and benefits and perks that reflect women's concerns. And they want the freedom to behave differently from men.

The reason culture clash generates sexual static is that it challenges male values and behaviors. Until recently, those in the dominant culture did not have to think about the values of those in subcultures. Thus, men find the static created by the clash of cultures particularly irritating. They see the conflict as a zero-sum game. If women win, men lose. However, there is reason to believe that when competency wins, everyone wins, irrespective of gender. The clash of cultures, while confusing and troublesome, can lead to positive change if understood.

When you add culture clash to role confusion and garbled communication, it's easy to see why men feel bewildered and irritated working with women. It's no one's fault that sexual static permeates the air. It's not men's fault that they feel confused and annoyed, or women's that they feel frustrated. However, sexual static exists and is directly related to the underutilization of women. In order to avoid sexual static, men often find subconscious reasons to devalue women, which in turn serves as a justification for excluding them. It's that simple.

Talking about sexual static points us in the direction of change that can bring men and women together rather than tearing them apart. If we can learn more about how role confusion, garbled communication, and culture clash cause uncertainty and discomfort, perhaps we can minimize the amount of sexual static in the air. It may be emotionally satisfying to think that sexual static will disappear on its own as time passes and men and women get used to working with each other, but that isn't likely without the active participation of men.

Since men are the dominant group, they will have to remove the glass ceiling, and that will be difficult since for them it constitutes a floor—a feeling of security. But women cannot be expected to break the ceiling from below. Think of what happens when a pane of glass is hit from below—those beneath the glass get cut and bloody. That's why women are looking for new answers. One answer may be to reduce sexual static. When men recognize that the static they're experiencing can be minimized, they will be more comfortable working with women, and more likely to value and utilize their talents. For this reason, it is important to learn more about how men feel and how their feelings relate to the underutilization of women.

5

How Men Feel

In the cartoon strip *Sally Forth,* written by two men, a male executive says to a woman, "Look, I admit I'm a dinosaur. I go to all the sensitivity seminars, but it's hard to remember everything I can and can't say. I am so sensitized that now every time I talk to a woman at work, I worry I might accidentally say something offensive. What I want to know is how come men have to take seminars to learn how to talk to women, but women don't have to learn how to talk to men? What makes you think you don't inadvertently say things that offend us?"[1]

This comment reflects how many men feel about working with women. They sense they are under attack and they're not sure why. Age, religion, marital status, profession, ethnicity, skin color, and temperament all shape the way an individual male views women in the work environment. This makes it difficult to generalize about how men feel. Nonetheless, if sexual static is to be reduced, it is important to understand how men feel about women in work relationships, for it is men who have the power to bring about change.

There is a growing literature about men focusing primarily on the concept of masculinity and changing male roles.[2] Increasing attention is being paid to an issue raised by sociologist Talcott Parsons almost fifty years ago: "Only in very exceptional cases can an adult man be genuinely self-respecting and enjoy a respected status in the eyes of others if he does not earn a living in an approved occupational role."[3] In other words, men are defined by the work they do, and this strong link between what a man does and his self-image is germane to the issue of underutilization and the glass ceiling.[4]

Believing that gender flux, or the changing roles of men and women, is a major source of sexual static, I wanted to know why men feel uncomfortable with women in positions of power. To find out, I conducted a telephone survey of executive men across the country and asked them how they felt about the growing visibility of women in nontraditional roles.[5] The interviews were open-ended. I asked the men one question: "How do you feel working in an environment where there are increasing numbers of women?" After their initial response, I asked follow-up questions about their working relationships with the women in their organizations. I also tried to determine the intensity of their feelings.

A content analysis of their responses revealed two main patterns. One had to do with the four working relationships the men discussed. The other had to do with three issues that were implicit in their comments. The two patterns fit together. The four working relationships, while not mutually exclusive, were: *supervising* women, *working with* women as peers, *competing with* women, and *working for* women. Responses generally differed depending on the primary working relationship between the men and the women they mentioned. The three major issues were: *loss of power and control*, *loss of male identity and self-esteem*, and *increasing discomfort or sexual static*.

If we take these patterns as a starting point, it is possible to offer a framework for thinking about how men feel

"One day, while we were sleeping,
somebody changed all the rules."

"One day, while we were sleeping . . ." The Stanley Family by Barbara and Jim Dale. © 1990 Universal Press Syndicate.

when women play roles previously played by men. Though it is an admittedly preliminary framework, it enables us to identify male feelings in a way that sheds light on female underutilization. Keep in mind that the responses are those of Caucasian male executives, most of whom work in traditional hierarchical organizations where the one best model is alive and well. Since I am aware that black men often feel differently from white men, I have also included a section on their feelings.

How Men Feel about Supervising Women

When men who primarily supervise women are asked how they feel, their most common response is "It's no problem." This is not surprising, since supervising women is consistent with traditional sex role expectations. Being in charge is what men are supposed to do. As supervisors, they still have power and are in control. Their self-image as males is in no way challenged. Their self-esteem remains intact. However, they do report an increase in sexual static. As one of the men I interviewed said, "There are more women, thus a greater number to sexually harass." He didn't mean he saw a greater opportunity to harass women but rather a greater possibility that some aspect of his behavior could be perceived as harassment.

Frank Harris, who manages a branch of a large bank in a southwestern city and has always supervised women, echoes this sentiment. "Today I feel tense with the women I supervise. I used to ask the cashiers or my loan officer out to lunch and think nothing of it. Today I feel uncomfortable doing so. Will they think I'm interested in them romantically? Do I pay or don't I pay for their lunch? I used to put my arm around women with whom I worked as a gesture of friendliness. Now I wonder if that's okay. I used to comment on the clothes one woman in particular wore because I wished my wife would wear what she wears. Now I suspect that's inappropriate. I find I'm not able to be myself because I'm not sure what I'm supposed to do." Because Harris has power over the women he supervises, he feels particularly vulnerable. The new rules are not clear, and ambiguity about what constitutes sexual harassment makes men like Harris uncomfortable and anxious. They know that as the headline of a *Wall Street Journal* article proclaimed, "A Hug by the Boss Could Lead to a Slap from the Judge."[6]

Another common feeling among men who primarily supervise women is that family support programs constitute a special privilege for women, even though the 1993 Family Leave Act provides parental leave for men too. This is another source of sexual static. Men don't take advantage of the law because they know they will be viewed as lacking commitment if they do. Eastman Kodak provides seventeen weeks of unpaid time off for men and women after the birth or adoption of a child, but over a four-year span few men participated in the program.[7]

Men are embarrassed to say they are taking time off from work for something as "unmasculine" as child care or tending to an elderly parent. Men who want to balance work and family feel frustrated and afraid of appearing less committed to their jobs. In an op-ed piece in the *New York Times*, Colin Harrison said, "The fact is, men's roles have changed less than we think. If anything, there is greater pressure now on men. The culture rightly asks that we be supportive husbands and devoted fathers. I'm afraid I would secretly look down upon a male co-worker who took a long parental leave as someone who was less serious about his work."[8] Some men resort to lying to avoid being stigmatized, like the man who told his boss he had another meeting rather than admit he was taking care of family responsibilities.[9] Yet women are also stigmatized when they take advantage of parental leave. Men conveniently forget this when they claim women have an unfair advantage because it's considered okay for them to attend to family responsibilities.

Taking time off for family reasons continues to be problematic for women, but it's particularly troublesome for men. Ironically, while executive men are reluctant to take parental leave for fear that their commitment will be questioned, and are often skeptical of women who take time off for childbirth, the time men take off for alcohol and drug rehabilitation programs, or for heart bypass operations, does not usually raise issues of commitment or special privilege. Yet there is evidence that male leaves of absence often have a severe impact on productivity.[10]

The men I spoke to also said they feel women are no longer content to be "helpers." They have the same kinds of career aspirations as men. They want to go back to school, to move from the "pink-collar" ghetto to the white-collar suburbs. They ask for time off to take special courses, reimbursement for attending conferences, professional counseling, and more challenging assignments. This bothers men who are used to women being happy in limited careers. Supervising women takes on a new dimension when women have new career expectations. It creates sexual static because men realize they can no longer depend on a lifetime of service from female subordinates. For example, executive secretaries, many of whom are high-paid professionals, no longer want to be called secretaries. They want to be "assistants" or "administrators." They hope ultimately to become something other than secretaries. Thus, some male supervisors give their secretaries the title "administrative assistant" in an attempt to make the women feel more like colleagues and prevent them from leaving.

The men's responses in aggregate paint a picture of male supervisors who feel the influx of professional women has not changed their sense of power and control. Nor has it materially affected their self-definition as males. It does, however, increase the amount of sexual static they experience.

How Men Feel Working with Women as Peers

It was not until the 1980s and 1990s that well-educated women with experience could be found in any numbers in most male-dominated occupations and professions. That is why the responses from men who work with women as peers came as no surprise. They said, "It's a new experience!" As the men talked, it became clear not only that it was a new experience but that their feelings were neither positive nor negative. They talked about the excitement of working with women but also about having to reexamine their own behavior because women seem to operate differently from men. Their responses can be interpreted as evidence of a slight decrease in their sense of power and control and some questioning of their self-definition as males.

My respondents' comments are consistent with how men think about the contribution of women at work. When I ask men to write down the qualities they feel women bring to the workplace, they most often list these.

Qualities Men Feel Women Bring to Work

- Different perspective/insights
- Sensitivity
- Compassion, caring
- Willingness to work hard
- Attention to detail

What this list tells us is that overall men feel women bring positive qualities to work, although some might consider attention to detail a negative. Yet when men are given the choice of working only with men or with men and women, they seem to prefer working with men. In 1987 a colleague and I conducted a pilot study of male and female audit teams in three large California public accounting firms. In-depth interviews of CPAs who ran the gamut from associates to managing partners revealed that the women preferred to work on mixed (male and female) audit teams and the men did not. The male CPAs overwhelmingly preferred all-male teams even though they expressed positive views about women in the workplace and volunteered that mixed audit teams were probably more innovative than all-male teams.[11]

Why was this the case? There are several answers. For one thing, there is comfort in sameness. It is easier to communicate with people who are like you, because you can understand and predict their behavior. There is less chance of saying the wrong thing or making incorrect assumptions. Another answer has to do with the understandable desire to minimize cognitive dissonance, or in this case, the inconsistency between the men's preference for all-male teams and their positive attitudes toward women and mixed teams. Cognitive dissonance is common in the workplace because of changing sex role expectations. In addition, when women assume positions of power, they often question the policies and practices of their organizations. They want decision making to be more inclusive, meetings to be less structured, benefit packages to be more flexible. In the face of such questioning, men feel a loss of power and control because they are forced to justify ways of doing things that they have always taken for granted.

Thus, while the responses of men who work with women as peers seem neither positive nor negative on the surface, upon further analysis there appears to be a more complex message. It cannot be assumed that because men and women work together in pursuit of common organizational goals, power and control issues disappear. Men are used to competing for power and control with other men, but not with women. As one of the male respondents said, "Because women see things differently, I sometimes feel at a disadvantage working with them. I begin to question my own thinking." In a very subtle way, female peers may challenge a man's self-image. The image of men as "those in the know" is so deeply rooted in our culture that when men are confronted with credible female ideas, they begin to assess their often unconscious assumption of male superiority in the domain of ideas. In the field of medicine, for example, female physicians and academics have called for major changes in medical school teaching and curricula, and male doctors are taking note. In manufacturing, the needs and preferences of women are changing product designs. In the military and religion, the idea of women as leaders has gained legitimacy. But none of these changes are painless for men.

At the same time that men report only a minimal loss of power and self-esteem working with women as peers, they describe a pronounced but not unwelcome increase in sexual tension. "There is an excitement that differs from working with women as subordinates," a senior executive in a major advertising firm told me. Sharing intellectual pursuits with women adds a dimension to the male/female relationship that the men said they often don't experience with their wives or female subordinates. Such feelings often lead to office romances and affairs, which can create serious problems at work if they turn sour.

When men and women work together on projects or important committees, they spend a lot of time with each other. They eat meals together. They go on trips together. They attend conferences together and stay at the same hotels. This heightens the sexual tension that accompanies working relationships. The uncertainty about how to handle office romance, or sexual matters in general, causes a considerable increase in sexual static for men who work with women as peers, (and for women too), and is even more troublesome for men who compete with women for positions and promotions.

How Men Feel Competing with Women

It's one thing to work with women as members of an audit team, as designers of a commercial building, as developers of a strategic business plan, or as part of a market research group or government legislative committee. It's another thing to compete with women for task assignments, career opportunities, or financial bonuses. That's probably why the general response of men who have competed with women was anxiety and confusion. While few used the word "anger," I could hear it in their voices. "Men aren't used to competing with women at work, and they don't feel they should have to," said one of the executives I interviewed. As Professor Thomas Kochman says, "White males have a sense of entitlement. They are like the first born in the family. They have the love of both parents and they are not quick to forgive the second child (i.e., women) for being born."[12] Men are surprised to find themselves competing against women, whom they have rarely seen as competitors. A cartoon in a woman's magazine shows a man complaining to another man, "So I tried to make a pass at the cute little blond walking around the office, and she fired me on the spot." The message is that it seemed impossible that a woman could have the power to hire and fire. Most men admit that they are still calling the shots, but they worry that they may not be much longer.

The discomfort men feel competing with women underlies the phenomenon of "white male backlash." Not only do men find competing with women a new experience but they sometimes feel that they, not women, are the victims. The backlash is manifested in a variety of ways. Often it is related to the emergence of large numbers of women, whose presence changes the dynamics in a group. For example, political scientist Lyn Kathlene found that as the proportion of women increases in a legislative body, men become more verbally aggressive and controlling in committee hearings. When there are only a few women, they may not be as threatening, and the men may be more likely to pay attention to them.[13] This finding seems inconsistent with the belief that as more women are elected and sit on policy-making groups, their power will increase. However, the issue of backlash when women assume positions of power in great numbers has not yet been examined in a corporate context, for it hasn't taken place.

Men's most common complaint about competing with women is that it is unfair. They firmly believe women get promoted because of affirmative action or special preferences. Larry Crabtree, a former manager with Wells Fargo Bank in California, admits that even when a clearly competent woman gets promoted over a male, men find themselves denying that the promotion was based on merit. Interestingly, men don't seem to regard preferential treatment based on being a golfing buddy or an old friend, having seniority, fitting in, etc., as unfair to women. When I asked Crabtree what he would think if he lost a promotion to a man he considered less qualified than he is, he said, "I'd call it a mistake!" His remarks were an honest assessment of what most men probably feel. It is easier for them to rationalize losing to a man than to a woman.

Women are familiar with the allegation of reverse discrimination to explain their career advances, but they say that men have nothing to fear but fair competition. Women understand that men have what Peggy McIntosh calls "an invisible package of unearned assets which can be cashed in each day like a knapsack of special provisions, assurances, tools, maps, guides, code books, passports, a compass, emergency gear and blank checks."[14] Most men are not conscious of their knapsacks. They have never had to think about how the knapsacks have provided men a jump start at work. Women, on the other hand, understand the power that these knapsacks contain, and all they're asking is that men give up their knapsacks or stop complaining when women pack knapsacks of their own.

Aware that men are having difficulty competing with women, a number of large corporations, among them AT&T, Motorola, Corestates Financial, and Du Pont, have instituted programs to help men explore their feelings.[15] The fact that the workplace is less secure in the prevailing climate of downsizing and reorganization intensifies male feelings of anxiety related to competing with women. On the one hand, this heightened level of male anxiety seems warranted since men lost a net 93,000 management jobs and women gained a net 520,000 between 1982 and 1992, according to a study by the *Wall Street Journal*.[16] On the other hand, men continue to hold many more management jobs than women, and it will take women thirty years to reach parity with men at their current rate of advancement. Women often wonder why men are so worried.

When I'm asked if my male M.B.A. students today are different from those who graduated fifteen years ago, I say yes and no. Today's young men know they will be competing with women throughout their careers. They point to the fact that they have competed with women in school for grades and elected positions, and say they're not concerned. I asked one of my students whose wife was in the same class (they were both engineers) how he felt competing with his wife academically and professionally. He said it was no problem. However, when she did better than he did on a class paper, I noticed him flinch when he looked at the grades. It is difficult, even for a modern man, not to mind losing to a woman, much less a wife! So while young men say competing with women doesn't bother them, I suspect that's because they have not yet competed for high-level positions. Let's face it. Competing with women flies in the face of what men have been taught.

When young men find themselves in competition with women in the workplace, they feel like their fathers felt; they have traditional role expectations for women. Ultimately, they realize that competing with women in a college setting is not the same as competing for a top position. As Joe Bob Briggs says in *Iron Joe Bob,* "Men have lost touch with their Spears, their Maces, their Battering Rams."[17] Today's arena of combat is the workplace. Men are supposed to do battle with other men, not women. And they are supposed to win. They, not their wives, are supposed to be the providers and protectors.

Many women today are advancing more rapidly in their careers than their spouses, and often this causes marital problems as well as lowered male self-esteem. Most men and women still believe that the husband is supposed to make more money than the wife. As a woman quoted in the *Wall Street Journal* said, "We weren't raised as women to think we were going to be married to a loser."[18] This traditional belief gives many men a sense of well-being, because they equate their earning status with power at home and at work. Yet in 1993 women in 21 percent of all dual-career marriages had higher incomes than their spouses. This reality adds to male discontent. On the other hand, men whose wives make a great deal of money may not feel threatened at all. On the contrary, they seem to enjoy it. Mike Nichols, a famous movie director and actor, no doubt has a substantial income. However, when his wife, TV anchorwoman Diane Sawyer, received a multimillion-dollar pay package from ABC, he was asked how he felt, as though it would upset him or make him jealous that his wife earned so much. He smiled and said he thought it was terrific. He was probably being truthful, since his male identity was not challenged, nor his feeling of self-esteem. Similarly, blue-collar men who know that what their wives make is needed to supplement their income may also be pleased with a wife who earns a good salary or hourly wage.

It is middle-management professional men on the way up the corporate ladder who are most often troubled by competition with women. It is they who feel the rules of the game have been changed. It is they who most often cry foul play when women advance. These men don't like to believe that women can also "make the cut." To them, women only make the cut because they're given a head start. When they see their wives doing as well as or better than they're doing, the sense of unfair competition is reinforced.

Men's major source of self-esteem is closely tied to what they do—their job and the income it generates. For reasons of biology as well as history, a woman's self-definition has to do with home and family. Men have had to create their self-definition and their sense of home through work. Man's primary home is his workplace. It is there that men spend most of their waking hours. It is there that they put their feet on the table and say whatever they want. It is there that they exhibit the learned behavior of males: competing in a game where the rules are well known and code words and behaviors are understood. Since the Industrial Revolution men have been defined as economic providers, those who pay the mortgage and taxes and put bread on the table. No longer can they do this alone. In most cases, spouses work because a second income is necessary. Thus, men feel they are not able to provide in the way they once could. It's bad enough to experience a sense of loss about being the sole provider, but on top of that, men feel that women are invading their home, which was once an all-male domain. And along with the loss of home, the invasion brings a loss of control, a blurring of self-image, and an increase in sexual static.[19]

The sexual static men encounter when they compete with women differs from the kind they feel when they mostly supervise or work with women as peers. It involves the added confusion of having to deal with competitors they have been trained to woo, not defeat. This is a significant source of male anxiety. Many men report feeling manipulated in a sexual way when they compete with women. They feel that women play by different rules, that they use their "feminine ways" or feign helplessness in order to appeal to the male ego— theirs or perhaps the boss's. In other words, they feel that women can endear themselves to men in ways they cannot. Men also feel that women are better at relating to others on a personal level, something they find difficult. They have trouble sorting out their feelings of sexual tension, competitive drive, confusion over how to compete, and anger at having to compete with competitors they believe have an advantage because they are female. Thus, men who compete with women report a major increase in sexual static.

How Men Feel Working for Women

We don't know much about how men feel working for women, because until recently there have been relatively few women supervising men at upper levels of management. However, among the men in my survey who had worked for a woman, the general response was "It depends on the woman." Some said they felt anger, anxiety, discomfort, and fear. Others said they loved working for women. The responses were in a bimodal distribution, meaning that they were at either end of a like/dislike continuum, with few feelings in the middle. This pattern may have more to do with the personal characteristics of the individual male respondent than in the case of the other three categories. Men with high self-esteem like working for women who use an interactive leadership style, because it gives them a sense of freedom. They say women are less likely to be concerned about power and status than male executives. Men with low self-esteem don't like working for women, because it reminds them of their feelings of inadequacy.

As men learn that women are capable of leading organizations and creating their own, they may subconsciously fear a loss of power for men. Here again it's a case of the zero-sum mentality, in which men lose when women win. When women occupy leadership positions, the organizational landscape changes. It becomes uncharted terrain for men, full of hidden bumps and potholes. Harris Sussman, a Massachusetts management consultant, says many men experience a sense of disorientation working for women because the top of an organization is where men make their last stand to be themselves and uphold what they think is the natural order of things. In Sussman's words, "Work is a male construct under siege." It's no wonder that some men don't like to talk about this issue, or deny their discomfort.[20]

Having negative emotions about working for a woman is one thing. Translating those emotions into action is another. Some women executives report that the men who work for them subtly try to undermine their effectiveness or challenge their competence. Others say that the men who work for them are supportive and helpful. Perhaps because having a woman boss is so new to men, their feelings about it do indeed "depend on the person."

In almost all cases, however, the men I interviewed ad-

98

mitted to a competency testing that takes place with women bosses but not with men. Often this testing stems from a feeling that women need to prove themselves because they are new as leaders, particularly in the corporate world. Competency testing (forcing women to prove themselves over and over again) is a manifestation of male fears about loss of power and control, as well as tarnished self-image. It is seen more often in men who work for women than in men who supervise, work with them as peers, or compete with them. Men who work for women need to reassure themselves that the women deserve their positions, because the link between masculinity and power remains strong.

Whether they find it a positive or negative experience, men who work for women report a type of sexual static somewhat different from that described by the other men. It's more complex, because the locus of control has shifted. It's the only instance where there's no doubt that the woman is in charge. This conflicts with basic notions of sexual power.

Joseph H. Pleck, a research associate at the Wellesley College Center for Research on Women, suggests that all men feel a need to exercise power over women. Pleck identifies three psychological roots of this need. The first is explained by the "mother domination" theory. Men feel the need to escape the control of their mothers by controlling other women. Thus, having a woman boss may remind men of the control their mothers had over them. Another factor is what he calls the "expressive power" women possess. He believes that many men are unable to express themselves emotionally and depend on women to help them do so. Pleck also speaks of the "masculinity-validating" power of women, by which he means that for men to feel masculine, women have to require them to act in a masculine fashion. This is what opening a car door or paying the bill at a restaurant is all about.[21]

If Pleck is correct that men associate women bosses with controlling mothers, that they are dependent on women to help them express their feelings, and that they need women to validate their masculinity, then it should be expected that when men work for women their sense of power and self-esteem goes down and the sexual static they experience goes up. Pleck suggests that if men reduce their dependency on women, their negative emotions toward them will be minimized. "Then men will be emotionally more free to negotiate the pragmatic realignment of power between the sexes that is underway in our society."[22]

As I said, not all men feel confused, anxious, or uncomfortable working for women. Some find it interesting, challenging, exciting, and a welcome change. These men say that working for a woman is better than working for a man because women tend to be well organized, less concerned about being right or doing things only their way, and comfortable sharing information, power, and credit. Some men say they feel empowered and relieved because women bosses care about how they feel and encourage them to express their feelings, which tends not to happen in male-led organizations.

Mike McNeil, a deputy for the Los Angeles County Sheriff's Department, told me how much he enjoys working for a female commander—a rare experience. He said her deputies feel free to bypass the traditional chain of command and talk to her when there are issues they want to air. Male commanders, on the other hand, always insist that deputies go through the chain of command, which often inhibits communication. Before this woman commander was appointed, it was not possible for a deputy sheriff to go directly to a commander. Now, he says, all deputies know they can go to the person at the top when necessary.[23]

Based on comments from the men I interviewed and from consultants who work with firms on gender issues, a few conclusions can be drawn about men who enjoy working for women. They tend to be secure in their jobs, they have high self-esteem, and they often have professional wives or daughters who are pursuing careers (which seems to be a good predictor of how men in general interact with women at work). These are the men who push organizations to find women for boards of directors and top-level positions. They are the ones who demand that all recruitment and promotion pools include women. They are the men least resistant to removing the glass ceiling. In fact, they are the ones most likely to insist on it. Conversely, men who are less secure in their jobs and have low self-esteem, troublesome marriages, difficulties with their mothers, stay-at-home wives, or no daughters tend to be the most uncomfortable working for a woman. This is not because these men consciously don't want to work for women but because their life experience has not prepared them to do so.

How Black Men Feel

As noted at the outset, the foregoing generalizations about how men feel are based on the comments of Caucasian males. Most black men feel differently about working with women. Although they are not in a position to change the climate in most organizations, it is important to talk about black men because their feelings indicate the complex nature of the intersection of race and gender.

Black men, like women, suffer from being compared to the one best model and coming up short. This leads them to be somewhat sympathetic to the underutilization of women: they know how it feels. At the same time, they believe that women have taken jobs away from them. They see the efforts of women to climb the corporate ladder as diminishing the chances for black men. They feel that women, particularly white women, are stealing the affirmative action spotlight. In other words, they see competition with white women as a losing proposition. If white women win, black men lose. "White women have become the minority of choice because white corporate America would rather have a white female than a black man," says Alphonso

Brown, a black management consultant and member of the Glass Ceiling Commission. Brown believes that of all the "minorities" white women are the least foreign to white men; thus, they are perceived by some as beneficiaries of affirmative action positions intended for black men.[24]

Black men also have mixed feelings about black women in the workplace. Although it might seem that they would be more sympathetic to black women than to white women, they sense that black women are also succeeding because white men prefer them over black men. Black women are seen as less threatening to white males than black men. Thus, black men feel disadvantaged competing with both black and white women.[25]

Black men constitute a significant subculture in corporate America because of their skin color. They may have grown up in the same country, gone to the same schools, played the same sports as the white males of the dominant culture, but they often encounter the same obstacles women face—always having to prove themselves, their advancement often no more than a token effort to meet pressures for cultural diversity. Even when a black man plays by the white male rules and is "white" in his values and aspirations, he can never remove the color of his skin and the prejudice it generates. In this respect, black men are in the same boat as women, since the two things we never forget when we meet people are their sex and the color of their skin. The cultural programming everyone carries around about sex and race remains at the core of the underutilization of women and people of color.

The Importance of Men's Feelings

Analyzing the responses of the men interviewed in my survey, and the many articles and books about men and male identity, we can summarize men's negative feelings about working with women as follows:

- Disorientation
- Confusion
- Irritation
- Anger
- Anxiety
- Tension
- Devaluation

Men's positive feelings can be summarized as:

- Excitement
- Empowerment
- Freedom
- Relief
- Sense of challenge

These feelings are consistent with the finding of Anthony Astrachan that men "feel more pain than pleasure about the changes women are making, and that the negative feelings are stronger than the positive."[26] If Astrachan is correct, it is important to understand why this is so. It is important to learn more about how men feel. If they don't feel comfortable working with and for women, change will take place slowly and women will remain an underutilized economic resource. If women are to be better utilized, men will have to value them, and the quantity of sexual static in the air will have to be reduced. This will only happen when men understand the complexity of their interactions with women at work. It will only happen when men feel that women's professional achievements do not detract from their own value.

"A long habit of not thinking a thing wrong gives it the superficial appearance of being right," said Thomas Paine in *Common Sense*. Duncan H. Spelman, a Caucasian male diversity consultant, says, "Because our race-gender group is the norm, we do not see how powerfully different the experience is for members of other groups."[27] It is not men's fault that they possess a special knapsack of privilege. Nor is it their fault that organizations are structured in a manner that facilitates white male dominance and rewards those who carry the knapsack. But that doesn't mean it isn't necessary to make men aware of their knapsacks so that they will eventually feel safe without them.

In the meantime it is also necessary to understand how women feel, and how they react to their feelings about the work environment. These reactions are analyzed in the next chapter.

6

How Women React

I'm told that Roseanne once said, "I know I'm a woman because I'm in charge of everything and everything is my fault." To many professional women, those words have a familiar ring. Though feelings differ from woman to woman, one thing is clear. It doesn't seem to matter if women are supervising, collaborating with, competing with, or working for men; they know their presence often makes men uncomfortable. They also know that being female, while sometimes a plus, can often be a minus in the work environment.

It's not difficult to learn about how women feel. The media is filled with stories of female accomplishments and joy, as well as female frustration and discontent. Management consultants and human resource people who conduct organizational audits and focus groups have stacks of comments from professional women attesting to their feelings. Some women, often those whose behavior most closely resembles that of their male colleagues, say they have never experienced sexual discrimination. Their feelings are positive, and they don't feel underutilized. Others report differential treatment based on gender but feel it is an individual problem rather than an organizational culture issue. Their feelings are neutral, and they may not feel underutilized. Still others contend there is a great deal of sexual discrimination. Their feelings are negative, and they usually do feel underutilized.

There is considerable evidence that more women fall into the last two categories than into the first, and that women tend to feel more devalued and underutilized than men. As a result they often feel frustrated, marginalized, and angry. In general, women who harbor negative feelings tend to react in one of several predictable ways. Analyzing these reactions can help executives understand the importance of addressing the problem of female underutilization.

The Spectrum of Women's Reactions

Denial

The comments of Carleton S. Fiorina, network systems vice president for strategy and market development at AT&T, illustrate what is meant by denial. "I have never felt that my sex has been a disadvantage to me," she told *Business Week*. "There's a lot of discussion that men won't give adequate clout or power to women. Women share an equal burden for that. No one can expect to be handed power."[1] What Fiorina failed to note is that AT&T, her employer, was sued for sexual discrimination in the 1970s and forced to change its recruitment and promotion policies as part of a settlement.[2] So while she personally may not have experienced discrimination, it does not follow that it does not exist. Unlike Fiorina, many women admit that sex bias is prevalent in the workplace but don't believe it affects them. According to a survey conducted by Professor Faye Crosby, this "denial of personal disadvantage" is common among professional women: "Although women earn less than male counterparts and believe that discrimination is a social problem, only 8% feel shortchanged."[3]

Denying the existence of sexual discrimination places the blame for the slow advancement of women on women themselves rather than on the organizations in which they work. Often women who deny glass ceiling problems conveniently forget that they had powerful male mentors, were "free riders"—that is, beneficiaries of women who previously protested discrimination—or chose to ignore differential treatment. On the other hand, they truly may never have experienced discrimination, or recognized it as such.

Women who deny the existence of gender bias are the same women who avoid joining women's groups because they feel it will hamper their acceptance by male colleagues. They also feel they don't need the support of such groups. They want women to stop complaining, work harder, and learn to play the male game. Often the first to attain leadership positions in male-dominated organizations, these women are reluctant to talk about discrimination, glass ceilings, or sexual static because they feel their personal success proves that such barriers don't exist. Because they are frequently token women and are watched carefully, they may deny gender problems for fear of diminishing their credibility. They feel that becoming "one of the boys" means they have passed the competency test.

It's difficult to question a woman's feeling that she has not experienced gender bias. That's what she feels. Very little has been written about this issue, but an informal study I conducted convinces me there is still a great deal of gender bias, and a great deal of female denial.[4] The study participants were women entrepreneurs, most of whom had previously worked in male-dominated corporations. When I asked about the corporate climate in which they had worked, 80 percent said they "had to work harder than males to be advanced at the same rate," 50 percent said "women in my firm had less credibility than males," and 51 percent said they thought "men were uncomfortable working with women." Only 7 percent said that "men and women were treated the same." Taken together, these responses seem to indicate that the women had experienced gender bias or sexual discrimination of some type. Yet when these same women were asked to check off their reasons for leaving corporate life to become entrepreneurs, almost 50 percent said "to make more money," and 47 percent said "to have more control over my life." Only 11 percent said they left because of "sex discrimination" or "a hostile environment."

These findings are noteworthy because of their inconsistency. Why did the women admit they experienced differential treatment yet deny discrimination as a reason for leaving corporate life? What they seemed to be saying was that they experienced discrimination but that their reaction to it was not negative, or at least not negative enough to motivate them to leave. I'm not sure this is the case. I think the women felt it was more socially acceptable to say "I want to earn more money" or "I want to have more control over my life" than to say "I left the corporate world because of discrimination" or "I was tired of being sexually harassed." In other words, "pull factors," those that draw women out of corporate life, tend to be cited more often than "push factors," those that drive them out, perhaps because of the stigma attached to "complaining women." This interpretation is consistent with faculty exit interviews conducted on university campuses. Female professors rarely say that sexual discrimination is their reason for leaving, but in private conversations they report gender bias as a primary cause.[5]

The denial by women that gender bias exists has not received the attention it deserves. If women deny the existence of discrimination, whether consciously or unconsciously, they are not likely to support the changes needed to eliminate it. In this context, denial is a negative reaction.

Collusion

Collusion is a reaction similar to denial. It is a kind of agreement that is not articulated. For our purposes, a colluder is someone who cooperates with "the system" in a way that reinforces stereotypic attitudes and prevailing values, behaviors, and/or norms.[6] In other words, women who collude "go along to get along." They may not feel good about discriminatory practices, but they don't want to speak up for fear of being considered outsiders. In essence, collusion is a survival strategy for women who think that if they protest they will be ostracized as troublemakers by their male peers. They remain silent, and in so doing support sexist and discriminatory behavior. Because collusion reinforces the status quo, women who collude are as guilty of discrimination as those with whom they collude.

Collusion is manifested in numerous ways. For example, if a sexist joke is made, a woman who finds it offensive may say nothing or even laugh. In this way she appears to agree with those in the dominant group. Men too can be colluders. In fact, it is usually more difficult for them not to collude, since they are a part of the dominant group. Because women are outsiders, they collude to become insiders. Because men are insiders, they collude so they can stay inside. Collusion, for both men and women, in many ways amounts to accepting discrimination as a necessary evil.

Acceptance

Acceptance of gender discrimination also takes a variety of forms. Some women express their acceptance by buying into the mommy-track philosophy that women with family responsibilities should agree to a slower rate of career advancement. That is, they accept the male belief that women can't balance work and family in a way that enables them to compete equally with men, so they shouldn't try. This justifies their underutilization.

Other women subscribe to the pipeline theory, which suggests that it is only a matter of time before women will fill the previously all-male pipelines leading to positions of power. These women are patient. They believe their day will come. However, their theory is suspect, since the pipelines have been filled with women for some time. Like colluders, women who believe in the pipeline theory are rarely motivated to undertake actions to change their work environment. They believe that gender bias will disappear in due course, so they decide to wait.

Acceptance of gender discrimination sometimes gives way to anger and action. In such cases, we can say that it was only "temporary acceptance." Sometimes women accept the glass ceiling until they bump their heads so often they find themselves with a continual headache and decide to act.

Challenge

When women can no longer tolerate gender bias, they challenge the status quo. They usually do this on one or more of four levels. On an *individual level*, they speak out and question policies or practices in their own unit or organization. The behavior of Carolyn Morris, formerly marketing manager for the Hewlett-Packard (H-P) 3000 computer, illustrates this type of challenge. She decided she didn't want to climb the corporate ladder alone, so she started a women's group within H-P. As an individual representing the sentiments of the group, she went to one of the company founders and told him she felt women were not being fully utilized at H-P. She waited and hoped things would change. However, her challenge went unheeded, or at least change didn't come fast enough for Morris. She left H-P and started her own company, Max West.[7]

On a *group level*, women often meet informally to discuss mutual experiences and provide emotional support for each other. Such groups are not always sanctioned by the organization, and often don't meet on company time. They tend to spring up as women talk to each other and discover common concerns that lead them to raise questions about their work environment. Lunches and planned social events create a bond between women who may previously have thought they were the only ones who felt devalued. Informal groups tend to be profession- or unit-specific. That is, women who have similar jobs or work within one division find each other and arrange to get together.

On an *organizational level*, women develop formal groups that are often offshoots of informal groups. Their purpose is to bring about change in the whole organization rather than in one unit or with respect to a specific job category. At American President Companies (APC), a large international shipping firm, Linda Cyrog-Giacomi, vice president of strategic marketing, and Pat Porter, director of international human resources, organized such a group in 1991, hoping to motivate APC executives to address gender issues. After informal discussion, Cyrog and Porter were asked by senior management to form a task force that would draft a business plan outlining the changes needed to enhance the career opportunities of women at APC.

It is worth describing how the women at APC challenged the company's corporate culture, because their challenge was successful.[8] They formed what they called the Women's Council, which was composed of a number of task forces that identified problems and suggested solutions. Since 1991 the efforts of the council have been impressive. A number of positive changes have taken place. Today it is the exception rather than the rule to see a major team or corporate initiative that does not have female representation. The first woman has been appointed to the APC board of directors. A woman has joined the six-member senior management group. The new vice president of human resources is a woman who replaced a man. The company now has its first woman regional vice president, as well as four female vice presidents—an increase of three in the past five years. John Lillie, chairman and CEO of APC, confirms the value of the council's work: "The Women's Council originally was formed to better the working environment and opportunities for women at APC. It's accomplishing that objective. Also, by example and by initiative, it is helping to achieve that objective for all employees at APC, the most specific result being the creation of a Diversity Initiative aimed at improving the work environment for all APC employees."[9]

On a *societal level,* women act on their feelings by joining statewide and national professional organizations that address gender issues, or by attempting to change societal or professional values. During the last decade, there has been an explosion of female professional associations in fields such as law, engineering, accounting, public relations, commercial real estate, education, and medicine. Such groups have well-established networks and increasingly act as advocates for legislation dealing with gender issues in their profession. They are perceived as a major force in bringing about change in the workplace. A number of these groups testified before the Labor Department's Glass Ceiling Commission when it held hearings in major cities across the United States in 1994.

Women's World Banking is challenging the traditional banking community, which rarely services low-income women. Nancy Barry, formerly with the World Bank, joined Women's World Banking as president in 1991. She felt that the structures, cultures, and people of traditional banks did not provide adequate opportunities for women, either as employees or as customers.[10] This New York not-for-profit financial institution was established in 1979 to advance and promote the full economic participation of women. Its goal is to create innovative instruments, new relationships, and effective systems that give poor women entrepreneurs access to banking services, markets, and information. The bank began as a local-global organization with most of its accounts in underdeveloped countries. It has a 99 percent repayment rate on the loans it has made and guaranteed to poor women. Today, recognizing the need to address the economic improvement of women in the United States, the bank is embarking on a program to apply the strategy of collaboration that has been so successful abroad to low-income women here, starting in New York and Los Angeles.

Challenging the status quo on all levels is having an effect. However, for some women, trying to break the glass ceiling from below is simply too painful. They react differently—they decide to flee!

Flight

When women decide that their challenges from within are not recognized, taken seriously, or acted upon quickly enough, they leave. They may move to a smaller, more hospitable organization, or they may start one of their own. Either way, by leaving they send a message that they don't feel valued or fully utilized.

Dr. Frances Conley, professor of neurosurgery at the Stanford Medical School and Hospital, is an example of a woman whose reactions changed over time from temporary acceptance to challenge to flight. After two decades on the Stanford faculty, she tendered her resignation, announcing that she could no longer put up with the pervasive sexist behavior and gender discrimination in the medical school and hospital. She said she felt she had been undervalued for too long and was fed up with what she called harassment and an "old boy" culture. The last straw was the dean's appointment of a new department chair. Dr. Conley contended that this man was a major source of the harassment and discrimination problems, and said she could not remain at Stanford with him as her boss. Her resignation made national headlines and forced Stanford administrators to examine male bias in the medical school. Only after the appointment had been rescinded and Dr. Conley had been assured that the administration would address the gender issues she had raised did she return to her faculty position.[11] Today the medical school is paying attention to improving the environment for women.

Women also flee to start their own organizations. Joline Godfrey, in *Our Wildest Dreams*, recounts numerous stories of women who took this path.[12] One story is her own. In 1986, after a decade as a "good corporate woman," Godfrey left the Polaroid Corporation to start her own company in Boston. An article in *Inc.* magazine a few years later made her angry, and the letter to the editor she wrote in response turned into *Our Wildest Dreams*, a book that documents the stories of women entrepreneurs across the country. Many of the women she writes about were also galvanized to start their own companies. Some were frustrated by corporate torpor, like Ruth Owades, who left a large direct-mail company in Massachusetts after the CEO told her that her idea for a catalog for home gardeners would never work, and who has since become the successful entrepreneur behind *Gardeners Eden*, later bought by Williams-Sonoma, and *Calyx and Corolla*, the innovative fresh-flower mail-order catalog. Some were impatient with corporate inflexibility. "When I worked in a large corporation and wanted to see my son's softball game I was called unprofessional," one respondent told Godfrey, "but now that I own the company no one ever calls me unprofessional." Some simply despaired that the glass ceiling would ever crack enough to let them through.

In 1992 there were an estimated 6.5 million female-owned businesses in the United States, employing more people than were employed in the Fortune 500 worldwide. In the early 1990s, when the largest U.S. companies were reducing their workforce, 25 percent of female-owned businesses were adding employees. Today almost half of all new businesses are created by women.[13] There are many reasons for the great increase in female-owned businesses, but one of them is certainly the negative experience of women in organizations that don't value them. In reacting to feelings of frustration and anger by becoming successful entrepreneurs, women talk with their feet.

Legal Action

Not only do women walk out on organizations, they also walk into courtrooms. Ann Hopkins is a well-known example. She sued her employer, Price Waterhouse, a large public accounting firm, after being passed over for a partnership in 1983. Her court case lasted seven years. In 1990 she finally won. The court ordered that she be made a partner and awarded her $371,000 in back pay.[14] The Hopkins case is telling. In every way, especially "rainmaking" (the generation of revenue), Hopkins was judged equal to or better than the men with whom she competed for a partnership position. As her legal case developed, depositions revealed that the men making the partnership decision thought she was "too aggressive." Rarely do men not make partner for this reason. The courts agreed. The Supreme Court upheld a lower-court ruling that Hopkins had been discriminated against because of her sex. Price Waterhouse suffered from negative publicity, and women's groups across the country cheered. Hopkins's legal action struck a blow against gender bias.

The Feelings and Reactions of Black Women

It should be stressed that the observations above do not reflect how all professional women feel, particularly women of color. Too often it is assumed that the experience of Caucasian women is the same as the experience of women of color. But while all women share some experiences by virtue of being female, women of color have very different stories to tell. For example, when asked about the problems they encounter at work, women of color often refer to a "Lucite ceiling" or a "concrete ceiling."[15] Women of color believe they are doubly discriminated against, because of their race as well as their gender—the "double whammy."[16] It is often difficult for black women to know whether they're being devalued because of their skin color or their sex.

Ella Bell and Stella Nkomo have studied the issue of race and gender for a number of years. They are adamant that although the combination of race and gender makes the underutilization issue even more complicated and perplexing in the case of women of color, it does not justify viewing gender issues in the context of white women alone.[17] They admit that career opportunities for black women are improving, as are those for white women. However, in many instances black women are being offered positions no longer sought by white women—in human resources, minority relations, and other occupations where they are expected to represent the concerns of minorities. And whatever positions they hold, they often feel like tokens under a microscope.

Black women also experience a different type of backlash than do white women. As the other side of the double whammy coin, they're often seen as "twofers."[18] In other words, if it is believed that for affirmative action purposes an employer gets two points by hiring a woman of color—one for gender and one for race—then the employer is getting two for the price of one. Michele Hooper's experience is a flagrant case in point. A corporate executive at Baxter International, Hooper was invited to join the Young President's Organization (YPO), a very prestigious group of mostly white male CEOs. She was introduced at a YPO dinner with the following comment: "It is good Hooper is a woman and even better that she is black—but it would have been best of all if she were disabled, also."[19] This mentality certainly exists, and some even claim that black women are doubly advantaged rather than doubly burdened by their race and gender, but Natalie Sokoloff, who has studied black women in the professions, says that this alleged "twofer" advantage is a myth.[20] It is one of many myths that flourish when gender intersects with race or ethnicity, creating problems for women of color that white women don't face.

The Importance of Women's Reactions

However women react to their feelings of being devalued and underutilized, their reactions affect the organizations in which they work. Unfortunately, the effects are not always as positive as those that followed Dr. Conley's resignation. Moreover, women's reactions are sometimes translated into physical and psychological tensions related to absenteeism, low morale, and a decrease in productivity.[21] These are the most obvious costs of devaluing women, black or white. Although there is little hard data to show a causal relationship between how women react and these symptoms of underutilization, common sense, as well as the extensive literature on "burnout,"[22] suggests that such a relationship exists.

What happens in organizations where such symptoms are not seen because women are valued? What difference does it make when organizations really utilize their women? In other words, what impact do women leaders make? The next chapter provides some answers.

117

7

The Impact Women Make

Judith Rogala is currently an executive vice president with Office Depot, responsible for revenues of well over $1 billion.[1] Wherever she has worked, she has left a trail of interactive, participatory management and higher profits. Wherever she has managed, her subordinates and peers have been quick to praise the way she respects, empowers, and motivates those with whom she works. Rogala's story is noteworthy because she has been a leader both in large, hierarchical, publicly held, male-dominated industries and in several small privately held firms.

Rogala spent twenty years with TWA, starting as a flight attendant and advancing to the general managership of Pacific Northwest regional operations. In 1980 she was hired away from TWA by Federal Express, where she worked for ten years. As a senior vice president at Federal Express, she was one of very few women in top management. In that capacity she controlled an expense budget of $600 million and a capital budget of $750 million, and supervised 19,000 employees. A number of these employees followed her in

1990 when she was hired by Flagship Express, an aviation services company and cargo airliner, as president, CEO, and director.

As in the other firms Rogala worked for, the key executives of Flagship Express were male. In all three firms she created a work environment that minimized status differences. She eliminated company cars and special parking places. She increased employee input by establishing a direct hotline to her for the use of everyone in the firm regardless of title or function. During Operation Desert Storm she personally called the spouses of the military personnel transported to the Middle East by Flagship Express. She gave them as much information as she could, knowing that they were worried and had been left in the dark about where their loved ones were stationed.

In all three firms, when problems arose, Rogala converted them into learning experiences rather than occasions to criticize or punish. She provided training for all employees. She developed strategies to minimize misunderstandings and conflict and to get results. She brought people together to confront disagreements and provided a safe environment for them to work things out. That is, she made it clear that she wanted employees to feel comfortable being candid, and created an atmosphere that discouraged divisiveness. It was often a new experience for her employees to understand that relationships and team building were ingredients in getting the job done. Rogala also insisted that employees keep a balanced perspective on work and personal life, and encouraged them to be with their families at mealtimes.

Rogala's story shows how a leadership style that empowers people and fosters good working relationships can be effective even in organizational structures that operate on the command-and-control model. By virtue of her leadership style, Rogala has had a highly positive impact not only on the morale, productivity, and loyalty of her employees but on profits.

Until recently, because so few women have held key positions in large institutions, there has been little examination of the impact of women leaders. Moreover, "impact" is a complex concept. What exactly constitutes impact? How should it be measured? Is it felt differently by different people? Does it differ depending on place and time? It is not possible to address these questions of impact without raising the question of critical mass. That is, how many women does it take to make an impact? Can one woman make an impact, or does it take ten? "Critical mass" is a term that describes some threshold number linked to a point in time when some kind of change takes place. But is critical mass gauged by absolute numbers, percentages, or both? Is there a magic number or percentage? And how is change determined over time? Unfortunately, there are no widely accepted answers to any of these questions.

However, there is general agreement that sex ratios are important in understanding how decisions are made.[2] While women are striving for equality, it may be that numbers alone do not tell the whole story, but an increase in numbers does seem to make a difference. For example, in the United States Senate, two women out of one hundred members did not seem to have much of an impact; in 1994, with the addition of only five new female senators, the climate changed appreciably.[3]

A dramatic example of this change was the women senators' effort to deny a navy admiral a fourth star upon retirement because of his behavior during the Tailhook Convention, where female naval officers were sexually harassed. Although the women senators were not successful, they were able to convince more than thirty of their male colleagues to vote with them. Their campaign to reprimand the admiral by denying him a star became a national issue because of their ability to make it a high priority in the Senate. Had the women not raised the issue, chances are the public would not even be aware that this type of disciplinary action was possible. In this context, it can be said that seven women constituted a critical mass because they had an impact.

In the private sector, critical mass is similarly difficult to measure. There is a belief that it takes only three women in an executive suite or three women on a board of directors to make a noticeable impact. This "rule of three" has become a widely used measure of critical mass,[4] and describes a theory that evolved from a focus group of women executives at the Center for the New American Workforce at Queens College in New York. According to the center's study of women who serve on corporate boards, "One woman risks being dismissed as a token; two women have to be careful not to sit together for fear of threatening the men; but three women constitute a critical mass that makes it possible to act as a bloc."[5]

Granting the need to develop a better measure of critical mass, it is still possible to make some generalizations about female impact. My personal observation and an analysis of studies of entrepreneurs, government officials, and corporate executives leads me to suggest that the areas where women have the greatest impact are these: *male and female behavior*, *power relationships*, *agenda setting*, *management process*, and *quantity and quality of benefits*.

Impact on Male and Female Behavior

A story told to me by a female senior executive of a very large bank in California illustrates how the presence of women changes male behavior. This executive was asked to join the board of directors of a large midwestern corporation listed on the New York Stock Exchange. She was the first woman on the all-male board of twelve "good old boys." During the first meeting she attended, their comments were peppered with four-letter words and sexist jokes. The board members soon realized that their language was probably offensive to the new female board member, but they weren't sure how to behave. Noticing their discomfort, she told the men that the words they were uttering were not new to her and that she had heard the jokes before. Her remarks let them know that she found their language inappropriate, but her diplomatic manner lessened their discomfort. In subsequent meetings their language changed. They no longer punctuated their comments with references to gender and race, and the meetings took on a more professional tone.

Another example is the experience of Shirley Cheramy. By virtue of being the first and only woman to be an office managing partner, she became a member of her firm's management team. She says, "The biggest impact I had on the management team was my physical presence, which significantly raised the level of consciousness of the male members of the team about issues impacting our women staff members and our women clients."[6]

The presence of women in leadership positions has an impact on female behavior too, although in a different way. The first wave of female executives often made other women feel uncomfortable because they tended to act like men. Female subordinates received mixed signals about how to behave. Women who have assumed leadership positions more recently tend to send a message that it's okay to act like a woman, that it does not mean being seen as incompetent and won't hamper career advancement. The "queen bee," or woman leader who emulates men, is increasingly the exception rather than the rule. Nonetheless, as I travel around the country, I hear reports from female professionals who feel that women leaders treat other women poorly. Interestingly, one study has found that women who inherit companies rather than work their way to the top do not treat women subordinates well or promote women to management positions.[7] This may be one explanation for the phenomenon. I suspect that because of the high visibility of women leaders, who are still rare, when one or two treat women badly, all women leaders get painted with the same "hard to work for women" brush.

Nancy Woodhull, a Pittsford, New York, media futurist and one of the founding editors of *USA Today*, says that the paper would have been *USA Yesterday* had it not been for the involvement of women in its birth. She is convinced this had an effect on the behavior of all *USA Today* reporters and editors, male and female. At *USA Today* no one is pigeonholed or devalued for making a pitch for a woman's story. Every issue must contain at least one picture of a woman above the fold (the top half of the paper), a rule that would never have been approved had women not been included as policymakers. People who work at *USA Today* feel free to talk about women's issues along with other topics, knowing that it in no way detracts from their credibility. This freedom does not exist in most newsrooms across the country, where there are few women in top editorial positions and women's issues are still considered "soft news." Woodhull attributes the unique culture of *USA Today* to the fact that two of the five founding managing editors, and three of the seven founding planning editors, were women. There is little doubt, she told me, that having women in positions of power has had a lasting impact at *USA Today*.[8]

Impact on Power Relationships

As I have said, women tend to view and exercise power differently from men. Historically, women have not had the kind of formal institutional power men have had. For this reason, women tend to pay less attention to formal power relations than men. Many professional women have developed less traditional ways of exercising power regardless of their titles.

Conventional wisdom holds that women don't like power, that they don't want power, that they are not comfortable with power. Most professional women would disagree. Frances Coady, a senior executive at the International publishing firm Random House U.K., says she looks at power in relation to what she is doing. Power to her is desirable because it allows her to make her ideas about writers and books come to life. Power is instrumental, not an end in itself. She feels that "the sex of people at the top does make a difference. Women's attitudes about power are less political."[9]

Coady's comments are echoed by other successful women who say they see power not as a personal goal but as a tool to get things done. Susan J. Inseley, who was the highest-ranking woman in the U.S. auto manufacturing industry in 1992, heads Honda's engine plant in Anna, Ohio. She says that she spends a lot of time on the factory floor "listening hard to the real experts," as she refers to the firm's hourly workers and suppliers.[10] In acknowledging that those on the factory floor know as much as or more than she does, Inseley exhibits the kind of power sharing that women tend to prefer. Women change the power relationship between boss and subordinate, which gives those who traditionally feel powerless a sense that their contributions are valued.

Charlotte Beers is a top executive at the advertising giant Ogilvy & Mather Worldwide. Unlike her male colleagues, she feels very comfortable complimenting lower-level staff members in major presentations before clients.[11] When she does this, she creates the impression that the firm appreciates good ideas regardless of their source. She negates the idea that those at the top are all-knowing and all-powerful. Beers is another example of women's tendency to share power and information.

In the public sector, there has been a marked change in power relationships between male and female legislators. As one of the by-products of legislative term limits, now the law in numerous cities and states, there is greater opportunity for women to run for office. When they are elected, the "old boys' network" loses some of its power. Women join previously all-male committees, become committee chairs, and represent key legislative votes. As more women take office, the ticket to political success hinges less on being "one of the boys."

Though it is not as easy to see, a similar process is at work in the private sector. As organizational structures become more informal and less hierarchical, the corporate "old boys' network" also loses some of its power. Title and authority as sources of power give way to expertise and special skills. That means competent women are more likely to gain power previously denied them. Women today are issuing and canceling contracts, selecting law and CPA firms, and determining how budgets are developed and moneys allocated. Their new power profoundly changes their relationships with their male counterparts. And as they become more credible, they are given more respect and more power.

To say that women change power relationships by sharing power is not to say that male leaders do not also empower subordinates. However, in general women are less wedded to traditional power relationships. They are more interested in "power to" than in "power over,"[12] and less prone to covet power as an end in itself. Women understand how it feels to be powerless, and thus are more likely to empower others.

ethnic minority groups too

Impact on Agenda Setting

In the public sector, the impact of women on political agendas has been particularly noticeable on the federal level. One of the first legislative acts of the 1993 Congress was passage of the Family Leave law. The prominence of women in President Clinton's victory, and the election of women to the Senate and House of Representatives, clearly made family issues a high priority for the 1993 Congress. On the state level, female legislators are more likely to concentrate on issues concerning women, children, family law, and health care; male legislators are more likely to concentrate on issues of business, finance, budget, taxes, and transportation.[13]

It is no surprise that the Glass Ceiling Commission was created under a female secretary of labor, Elizabeth Dole. It is no surprise that it was a woman, Bernadine Healy, who brought the need to study women's health issues to public attention as director of the National Institutes of Health. It is no surprise that it was a female secretary of energy, Hazel O'Leary, who insisted that previously secret files on the exposure of American citizens to radiation be made public. And it is no surprise that Representative Patricia Schroeder, a member of the House Armed Services Committee, is the prime mover behind providing increased opportunities for women in the military. I am not suggesting that men are not concerned about women's issues. However, women clearly tend to push for and represent public policies that deal with health, education, welfare, and children.

Women also tend to change the way legislation is framed. Lyn Kathlene, who has studied legislators extensively, found that women are more likely than men to sponsor innovative legislation in the form of comprehensive, nonincremental bills. Women's bills often deal with new areas for public legislation, new solutions to old problems, and new kinds of programs. Men are more likely to change the legislative agenda incrementally by modifying or updating existing laws.[14]

The impact of women leaders on institutional agendas can also be seen in the field of education. After becoming dean of St. Mary's School of Law in San Antonio, Barbara Bader Aldave lost no time in changing the school's priorities and programs. She was quick to introduce such seminars as Women, Feminism, and the Law. She expanded the school's programs in public interest, environmental, and international law. She established legal aid clinics that allowed law students to earn credit for helping low-income clients. Her changes created controversy because they led the school away from its traditional mission of training lawyers in the technical aspects of the law.[15] This controversy was to be expected, for most major changes generate negative reactions. That's why it usually takes outsiders like women to initiate real change. They have little vested interest in the status quo.

In the private sector, many stories attest to women's impact on the corporate agenda. In the early 1990s, Jill Ker Conway, former Smith College president, was the only female member of the board of directors of Nike. Conway told the board that she thought the company's understanding of the female market was limited, and suggested that Nike create a women's division. Initially her idea was rejected out of hand. As Nike president Richard Donahue recalled, "Our habit was to take a male product, color it pink and sell it." Conway kept arguing for a separate division run by women and targeting female customers. Eventually the board acquiesced, and by late 1993 the women's division accounted for 20 percent of Nike's domestic revenues.[16]

Kate Bednarski, who eventually left Nike to start her own firm, also had a hand in getting Nike to focus on female consumers. She convinced Nike executives that there was an untapped market for women's athletic shoes. Bednarski knew that women's feet are different from men's, and that women needed an athletic shoe specifically designed for them. She also thought Nike needed an advertising campaign aimed at women. The company had been very successful with its ad strategy of associating its product with male sports heroes, but Bednarski felt this approach wouldn't work with women. Her male colleagues disagreed. Nike tried its male formula, substituting women athletes, and failed. Finally Bednarski was asked to develop a strategy aimed at women. When she presented her new ad campaign to the male executives—a series of statements about how women feel when they're told they can't do something because they are women, followed by the Nike slogan, "Just do it!"—the men were less than pleased. The women who watched the ads got shivers. The "Just do it!" slogan hit a responsive chord when connected with the familiar message to women that they can't do it. The men didn't get it, but Bednarski convinced them that although the ads did not speak to men, they spoke to women.[17] The rest is history. Her Nike ads won numerous awards and were the talk of the advertising community. Today Nike is perceived as a firm that cares about women. If Conway and Bednarski hadn't argued for changing its corporate agenda, Nike might be less profitable today.

A similar story can be told about the automobile industry, where women designers have been largely responsible for built-in children's car seats, safety belts that don't crease clothing, and door handles that don't break fingernails. It is clearly women who have pushed for female dealers and a recognition that the industry can no longer ignore the female market.[18]

Women also change the direction of the flow of corporate contributions and profits. Muriel Siebert, founder and president of Muriel Siebert Company, a large New York discount brokerage firm, and the first woman to purchase a seat on the New York Stock Exchange, shares her profits with charities that help women and the poor. "Instead of just shoving these commission dollars into my pocket, I decided to shove some of that money back into the community," says Siebert proudly. Through a program she calls the Siebert Entrepreneurial Philanthropic Plan, she contributes a percentage of her profits to charities in cities where her firm functions as an underwriter of bonds. When Siebert underwrote Chicago's water revenue bonds, the mayor of the city received half her profits to be used to help children and those in poverty. Siebert has changed the incentive agenda for the financial services industry. She has introduced a concept of commission sharing that has led others to follow. While investors don't receive tax deductions or save money trading with Siebert, they like the idea that they are making an indirect charitable contribution. Her idea of sharing profits, she says, will help the 1990s become a "decade of decency," unlike the 1980s, the "decade of greed."[19]

Nickelodeon's president, Geraldine Laybourne, is another woman who has changed the agenda in her organization. Aware that almost all children's programming has been aimed at boys, she is one of the first to make a concerted effort to develop TV shows for very young and teenage girls. In addition, her highly profitable cable company has been innovative in programming that is more than mere entertainment, in line with Laybourne's statement that "our goal is to raise a generation of young people who care about the world."[20] Profit is not Laybourne's only motive.

Impact on Management Process

When women are in positions of power, they tend to pay a great deal of attention to the way things get done. Their interactive style leads them to favor a consensual and collaborative process, a preference often attributed to the female concern for personal relationships.

Psychologist Carol Gilligan believes that women are more relationship-oriented than men because of psychological needs stemming from early gender identification with their mothers. She speaks of the relationship need of girls to be connected to their mothers as a way of being female, and the independence need of boys to separate from their mothers in order to be male.[21] Because of this difference, girls and boys tend to approach the world differently. For example, recent research shows that when girls play computer games, they are interested in the participative experience. They like verbal feedback, especially if it is supportive and focuses on their effort. They like flexible, open-ended activities, and they tend to change or ignore rules if they find them too constraining or artificial. Girls play until they get bored rather than until they win. Boys, on the other hand, focus on their scores and how well they're doing. They don't like feedback, but when they get it, they want it to focus on their ability, not their effort. They feel that praise for effort reflects negatively on their performance. Rules are important to boys because they establish who's the best. Boys play to win, not just to have fun.[22]

The distinction between the relationship orientations of women and men has often been used to suggest that women cannot exercise power effectively. Here again, "effectively" turns out to mean "like men." Because women are more relationship-oriented than men, they tend to exercise power differently but not necessarily less effectively. Women believe that when people feel good about themselves, they are more productive. The point here is that women's impact on organizations tends to differ from men's because they pay more attention to process, or how tasks are performed, and they prefer a different type of process. This does not mean women are not interested in outcomes. They are. However, they see a connection between a collaborative and participatory process and more innovative and profitable outcomes. Men tend to associate a top-down process with effective management.

Anecdotal evidence supports this view. In fact, much of the discomfort and sexual static men report in working with women is couched in terms of annoyance at women's preoccupation with process. As one male manager with a female boss said, "I'm sick to death of process. My boss is so concerned with process that it takes a long time to get to the outcome."[23]

In an experiment once recounted to me, groups of men and women were asked to solve a problem that had no specific answer. Each group was put in a room and given the problem and a set time to solve it. They were observed through a one-way mirror. A leader always emerged in the male groups, whose problem-solving process was top-down and competitive. The men rather quickly came to what they believed was the right answer. The female groups took far longer than the men to finish, and no one leader could be identified. The female process was participatory and looked chaotic to the viewer. The women generated five different answers rather than one, all in an if/then format. This experiment is significant in that it provides evidence of male-female process differences at a time when there is little hard data on the subject. There is no evidence that either of the processes is intrinsically superior to the other, but the collaborative process has benefits that have not been recognized in the past.

Susan Davis, president of Capital Missions Company of St. Charles, Illinois, believes that "collaboration is the highest form of competition." Companies, she says, are frequently more productive and profitable if they operate collaboratively. As an example, Davis points to the experience of those who participate in her Investors' Circle. The members of the Investors' Circle, a variety of people interested in funding socially responsible corporations, bring their best deals to each other for investment purposes. In so doing, they earn more profit than if they hoarded the best deals for themselves. In other words, they end up with parts of many good deals rather than a part in only one good deal. Further, they spread their risk by diversifying and leverage their "due diligence" capability by trusting the expertise of experienced peer investors. The collaborative process is relatively new in the venture capital industry, where intense competition for investment opportunities has been the model.[24]

In police departments across the country, the presence of women is altering the traditional way of processing criminal suspects. Women are increasingly recognized as particularly effective in coaxing alleged lawbreakers into patrol cars. They use a different arrest process from men; they tend not to raise their voices, or their batons. Male police officers have noticed this, and often ask to be paired with a woman because the female arrest process complements their own.

It's interesting that in the Los Angeles Police Department, Captain Margaret York and her partner have the highest confession rate in the entire city homicide division. As she explains her achievement, "These people either look at us as a mother figure, or they think we are too stupid to know what to do with the information."[25]

Women officers are also very successful in community-based policing, domestic violence cases, and working with juveniles. Hearing President Clinton's pledge to put a large number of new police officers on American streets in 1994, the chief of police of New Haven, Connecticut, told a nation-wide TV audience he felt all the new officers should be women. When asked to explain his statement, the chief said that because women officers are less confrontational, they are particularly effective in handling the urban conflicts that plague our cities.[26]

Gender differences about process are also reflected in the design of public policy. For example, male legislators tend to see crime as behavior for which individuals should take personal responsibility. Women see it as linked to larger societal problems. Therefore, the policy most often recommended by female legislators is to treat criminals in the context of poverty, poor education, lack of jobs, etc., and to call for preventive measures and long-term remedies, including rehabilitation. Male legislators are more likely to ask for strict punishments narrowly connected to specific criminal acts.[27] Texas senator Phil Gramm illustrated this distinction when he said that Janet Reno was a "very sweet lady" but "shouldn't be attorney general." He meant that her concern for childcare somehow detracted from her role as a prosecutor of criminals. "Child care is an important part of the puzzle," Gramm said, "but it's not her part of the puzzle."[28]

In the private sector, there are many stories about the impact of women on process. John Hunkin, president of the Canadian Imperial Bank of Commerce, participated in a corporate forum in which male and female upper managers talked about gender and leadership. After the session was over, they were given the task of organizing the ideas that had been presented. Hunkin said that this made clear to him the differences in the way men and women approach and solve problems: "Together the men came up with a list of points, and said, 'Fix them and the world will be perfect.' The women looked at how each point related to the whole problem."[29]

In the male-dominated funeral industry, the process of helping people cope with death has not changed much over the years. The image of an undertaker is a man in a dark suit talking in a low, solemn voice in a dreary formal setting. When Toni Gruerio took over her father's funeral home, that was the process she inherited. She decided to change the way customers were treated. She painted the funeral home in bright colors and did away with the impersonal atmosphere. She put up mirrors, believing that people like to look at themselves at a funeral because it reassures them to know *they* are still here. Gruerio created an environment that allowed her customers to grieve in whatever manner they wished. They felt free to celebrate a past life with loud talking and drinking as well as to mourn a sad event in quiet solemnity. Gruerio's female touch in the funeral business is perhaps a forerunner of things to come. It's an example of the impact of a woman in an industry where men have always been in charge. Although it is not known whether her profits increased (that's not public information), she says her customer satisfaction improved.[30]

Perhaps the most obvious impact women have on process can be seen in the area of communication. Kathleen J. Burke, former director of Human Resources and today vice chairman and member of the Managing Committee for the Bank of America, was responsible for the unpleasant task of eliminating twelve thousand positions after the bank merged with Security Pacific. Analyzing the task, she saw the need to develop a dialogue between employees and management. Knowing the fear and uncertainty caused by the merger, Burke urged bank managers to communicate often with employees and try to address their concerns. She personally sat down with many troubled workers to talk about severance pay and programs, and she walked them through the details.[31] She could have delegated these tasks to others, but she chose to do them herself. In this way she communicated her concern both about the downsizing process and for a profitable outcome, and received valuable feedback about employee morale.

Women also affect process when they take an interest in organizational learning. The field of medicine is a case in point. Until recently, medical schools used male cadavers almost exclusively for teaching purposes. This is no longer the case, although change has been slow. Dr. Adriane Fugh-Berman tells of her first day in medical school in the late 1980s, when a lab instructor told students to cut off the breasts of a female cadaver and discard them. The message was clearly that the female breast had little if any medical significance.[32] It may seem difficult to believe that this kind of teaching was alive and well in the late 1980s, but it was not unique. Until there was a critical mass of women in medical schools in the mid-1980s, few questions were raised about the process by which medical school learning took place. Rarely were women used in research trials, and it was assumed that what was true for men was true for women. The emergence of women's health as a medical issue can be directly tied to the impact of female students, female physicians, and female professors on the medical school teaching process.

All these examples show that women have an impact on processes that in turn can have a positive impact on outcomes. Some predict that as more women assume positions of power, interpersonal relationships, communication, and organizational learning will improve. Others suggest that women will become more like men and that a concern for outcomes will outweigh their concern for process. The assumption here is that those who do not have power are the ones who argue for a more open, interactive process, and that once in power the women will change, not the process. Only time and further study will tell if the female concern for process is related to being an outsider, being socialized as a woman, or some other factor.

Impact on the Quantity and Quality of Benefits

The most obvious impact women have when they assume positions of power is to call for new kinds of benefits. It is almost always women rather than men who ask for child-care and eldercare policies, flexible work hours, job sharing, cafeteria benefit packages, and nontraditional "perks." Jean Sisco, a woman who sits on eight corporate boards, says that women on boards of directors "are not shy about advocating policies that help women" and "are inclined to ask about the glass ceiling, about what is being done to recruit good women and encourage them to remain."[33] In a Catalyst survey of Fortune 1000 companies, 52 percent of the 162 women board-member respondents said it was their job to address work-family policies.[34] And one of the last bulwarks of male tradition, the United States Supreme Court, recently felt the impact of a woman in the area of benefits.

During her first year on the Supreme Court, Justice Ruth Bader Ginsburg was asked why she took the unprecedented step of agreeing to a flexible work schedule for one of her male law clerks. Since there were so many bright young clerks available to her, why should she choose to accommodate a male clerk who requested special hours so he could care for his child? Justice Ginsburg's response to her critics was pure female: "This is my dream of the way the world should be. When fathers take equal responsibility for the care of their children, that's when women will truly be liberated."[35]

The issue of balancing work and family has been brilliantly analyzed by Lotte Bailyn in *Breaking the Mold*. Bailyn makes the case that there is a need to change the mind-set about work and family as separate spheres. She says, "We need to find a way for employees to contribute to increased demands for productivity without neglecting personal needs or relying on gendered distribution of roles."[36]

The stories recounted above do not a theory make. However, they suggest that women do have an impact that can be attributed to their being female, and that their impact is positive. If this is true, how can organizations create environments that will facilitate a better utilization of women? In the next chapter I offer some answers.

8

Reforming Organizations

In her trailblazing 1977 book, *Men and Women of the Corporation*, Professor Rosabeth Kanter pointed out that large, traditional, hierarchical organizations handicap the careers of talented women.[1] Kanter took as one of her chapter epigraphs a quotation from Wilbert Moore's *Conduct of the Corporation*: "The corporation seems to seek an arrangement which is surely an anomaly in human society, that of homosexual reproduction."[2]

In an organizational context, "homosexual reproduction" means that white men replace other, similar white men when management changes are made. Kanter's analysis of this phenomenon demonstrated how most institutions operate to foster sameness and to exclude women from consideration as potential leaders.[3] She showed that women who made it to the top in 1977 were the exception rather than the rule. To a great extent this is true today, almost twenty years later.

However, as organizations downsize, form alliances with other organizations, and develop new types of services and markets, they find they have to be very flexible and adaptable to change. For this reason, as we have seen, questions of leadership and organizational restructuring have recently become important. At the same time, the types of changes women say would allow them to balance home and work, and to be more productive—e.g., job sharing, flexible hours, and telecommuting—are consistent with changing organizational needs. As we will see, the stages of organizational awareness about the need to restructure are in many ways similar to the stages of awareness about the need to address female underutilization.

The Wake-up Call

For most executives, addressing the underutilization of women has not been a high priority. Though they may be attuned to equal opportunity requirements, sexual harassment laws, and the cost of noncompliance with those requirements and laws, executives generally fail to link gender issues to their organization's bottom line. They may be mindful of a higher turnover rate for women than for men, or of the difficulty of recruiting and retaining women, but they see these as human resource issues, not major management strategy concerns. Most executives also fail to link the changes needed to utilize women more fully with the restructuring required and made possible by advancing technology as it collapses time and space.

In traditional organizations, managers can closely monitor subordinates because of their physical presence, often referred to as "face time."[4] However, in what is being called the "virtual corporation," where organizational boundaries are shaped by technology and collaborative networks of people rather than walls, the nature of control changes. Power and information are diffused. Women, because they tend to be comfortable sharing power and information, and less concerned about control than men, often adapt well to

138

this type of work environment. Thus, men may soon discover that their female peers can show them the way as they reengineer and reinvent their organizations.[5]

Wake-up calls about the underutilization of women come from a variety of places. Human resource departments, adult daughters, working wives, articles in magazines and newspapers, and speeches at professional meetings are common sources of these calls. Though reactions to the wake-up call differ from individual to individual and from organization to organization, the most common response is to turn over and go back to sleep. Fortunately, this is not the only reaction.

Anecdotal data, as well as the research Marilyn Loden and I did for our book on valuing employee diversity, support some broad generalizations about wake-up-call reactions.[6] One reaction, understandably, is fear. Change represents a challenge to the status quo. It raises the question of winners and losers. It creates a sense of uncertainty. Fear is usually negative, because those who feel fearful tend to:

- Avoid the issue
- Deny its existence
- Become defensive
- Become hostile

These reactions require no elaboration, for they are well understood and easy to see in many organizations today. Another reaction is confusion, which plays out in a number of ways. Sometimes it takes the form of a request for more information. For example, those who are confused may do the following:

- Generate discussion about why the wake-up call needs answering.
- Organize a task force to look into alleged problems.
- Use an outside consultant to assess whether there really is a problem.

Such reactions may suggest a genuine desire to become better informed. In themselves, these reactions are neither positive nor negative.

Another response of those who are confused is to re-define the issue. In some cases, this can be an attempt to shift attention from female underutilization in the workplace to an alleged female advantage in the workplace. This kind of redefinition casts the underutilization issue as a matter of "reverse discrimination" or "political correctness."

The claim that addressing the underutilization of women leads to reverse discrimination is an obvious attempt to obscure the disadvantages of being female by highlighting the purported disadvantages of being male. In other words, it is an effort to show that men become victims as women become victors. Those who complain about reverse discrimination argue that women are only hired or promoted because they are women, not because they are qualified—that is, because of affirmative action. While it is true that in some instances men may have been disadvantaged by legally mandated guidelines, in most cases women have had to be twice as qualified and work twice as hard as men in order to succeed.

Another way to redefine the underutilization issue is to talk about political correctness. Like the reverse discrimination argument, this shifts the terms of the discussion. It suggests that anyone who is concerned about utilizing the talents of women is an ideologue seeking to impose a rigid set of rights and wrongs on employers, often about such "trivial" matters as the use of certain words or the appropriateness of certain "natural" behaviors. "Political correctness," in my opinion, is an invention of the political right meant to stifle discussion of cultural diversity. Which is not to say that the political left hasn't inflamed the diversity issue while offering few constructive ideas. In any case, gender, as well as race and ethnicity, raises real workplace issues that are too often lost in the ideological passions aroused by accusations of political correctness.

Redefining the issue isn't always a negative process, however. In fact, this whole book can be seen as an effort to bring about a positive redefinition, one that prompts executives and managers to:

- Think about female underutilization as a bottom-line rather than a social equity issue.
- Think about female underutilization in the context of an overall change strategy rather than merely as a human resource issue.

Not everyone who receives a wake-up call is angry, fearful, or confused. Some are challenged. Those who react to the wake-up call as a challenge see the valuing and better utilization of women as:

- Increasing morale
- Generating innovation
- Improving profits

This response to the wake-up call recognizes that when women are valued, they feel better about their work, which translates into higher morale and increased productivity. It also recognizes that women tend to look at products and services differently from men, and that they provide insights and new ideas that lead to innovation, which leads to higher profits.

Obviously, organizations that react to the wake-up call in a positive manner, particularly those that see it as a challenge, are more likely to take action, and thus to benefit from utilizing women more fully, than are organizations that do not. However, it is naive to suggest that negative and positive reactions are mutually exclusive. Fear, confusion, and challenge often occur together in the context of the wake-up call. The question is, what happens next? What do organizations do after receiving a wake-up call? Is it possible to classify organizations according to stages of awareness and action? I think so."

Organizational Stages

Stage 1: Staying out of Trouble

In Stage 1 organizations, gender issues are seen in the context of compliance with affirmative action and sexual harassment laws and policies. These organizations respond to inside and outside pressures and alter recruitment and promotion practices primarily to avoid legal action. It is the law and the consequences of not abiding by it that impels them to think about how women are perceived and treated. Organizations in this stage are in essence saying by their actions, "We're staying out of trouble." They often hire outside lawyers who specialize in gender issues, or assign in-house counsel to advise them on what they must do to prevent legal difficulties.

Stage 1 organizations consider themselves successful if their legal record is good. In this stage, there is a "fix-it"

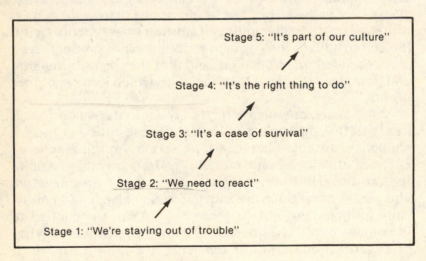

Stages of Awareness and Action.

mentality. Women are viewed as a problem rather than a resource. The one best model is alive and well, and it is assumed that if women don't advance at the same rate as men, it's because they don't work hard enough, long enough, or smart enough. There may be a few programs to raise awareness of gender issues or develop skills for women who feel they need them. There are usually no flextime policies, and women are primarily found in dead-end positions. Rarely are there women in real positions of power in Stage 1 organizations.

Stage 2: We Need to React

Organizations in Stage 2 realize that the second shift many women work at home causes them career/family problems not shared by men. Stage 2 managers begin to be aware of high female turnover rates, greater female absenteeism, and women's complaints about differential task assignments and stunted career opportunities. However, this awareness is seldom translated into action, and there is no concerted effort to do anything other than ensure compliance with affirmative action mandates. If human resource people attempt to convince top executives of the need for stronger action, the response usually indicates that gender issues are not a high priority. Stage 2 organizations may provide minimal training for women, and work/family concerns may prompt them to offer new kinds of benefits, but such changes generally take place only in the face of great pressure from female employees.

When Stage 2 firms launch national advertising campaigns, their ads tend to feature white males. Their annual reports, if they contain pictures of women at all, show them in support roles rather than as executives. Stage 2 organizations pay little attention to female markets, on the assumption that women and men have similar consumer characteristics. They also assume that qualified women will advance once they learn the ropes. In Stage 2 organizations, women still feel they have to think and act like men if they're going to succeed.

Stage 3: It's a Case of Survival

Executives in Stage 3 organizations realize that they have to react, so they take the next step and become proactive. They acknowledge that addressing gender issues is important not only for the women in the organization but for the organization as a whole. They agree that in general women are not given the same opportunities as men. They admit that women are often left out of informal meetings and events where men conduct business. Their consciousness has been raised, which is an important first step.

In Stage 3 firms there is usually a fair degree of training, but it is primarily aimed at helping women "fit" into the male culture. Training is seen as an add-on rather than an integral part of the organization's strategic planning. In other words, the emphasis is on programs to change the women rather than changing the organizational culture so it values female work behavior more adequately.

In many Stage 3 organizations there is at least one woman on the board of directors or in a top position. However, these women are usually not boat rockers; they tend to exhibit male values and behavior. The values of the dominant group are firmly in place, although annual reports probably include pictures of women in a variety of settings. There may be a smattering of female officers, but most likely in staff rather than line positions. Stage 3 organizations often have women's networks, councils, or mentoring programs that indicate some commitment to change, but top-level commitment is usually scattered and spasmodic. It rarely reflects an overall philosophy.

Stage 3 organizations have begun to view women in the context of the bottom line. They recognize women as an economic resource even though they may not be sure how best to capitalize on it. They believe that women bring a different viewpoint to work, a special way of leading, a different slant on how products and markets should be developed. They also recognize that women are in the workplace to stay, that they want careers, not just jobs. Executives whose organizations are in this pivotal stage know that if they are to attract and retain highly skilled women, they need to change their policies and practices. They agree with Jack MacAllister, former chairman of U.S. West, who said in 1987, "The world in which we live is far too competitive to pass up available resources. You'll not win races for long, firing only half of the cylinders in your engine. . . . In my opinion, the only way to be competitive is to use all of the talent you can muster, no matter how it is packaged."[8]

Stage 3 organizations realize that utilizing women more fully is related to their survival. They are not motivated to change for moral or social equity reasons. Rather, they are concerned about being able to compete economically. This shift to thinking about the utilization of women as a strategy for gaining a competitive advantage is the key to moving out of Stage 3 toward Stage 4.

Stage 4: It's the Right Thing to Do

By the time an organization reaches Stage 4, there is a top-level commitment to addressing the underutilization of women. Key executives have probably participated in some type of gender awareness training themselves and have allocated resources for extensive efforts to bring about organizational change. There is a genuine attempt to develop policies and practices that are inclusive rather than exclusive, and there are ongoing programs aimed at improving the work environment for women and other under-represented groups. Flextime and flexplace are accepted, and cafeteria benefits are likely to be available.

In Stage 4 organizations there may be a cultural diversity director with an assistant assigned to issues of gender, and there may be a newsletter that highlights issues of concern to women, people of color, gays and lesbians, and other groups. There are usually a number of women in top management who support the advancement of other women, and there is likely to be at least one woman on the board of directors. Stage 4 organizations pay attention to gender together with other diversity issues. Their commitment to change is firmly in place. Women want to work in Stage 4 companies because they know good career opportunities will be accessible.

Perhaps the most notable difference between Stage 3 and Stage 4 is that in Stage 4 organizations women are seen as a source of competitive advantage and female utilization is tied to managerial accountability. That is, managers are required to provide evidence that they are recruiting and retaining women at all levels, and to develop strategies for valuing women in their respective areas of responsibility. Rewards and bonuses are based on the achievement of well-defined diversity goals, thus providing a powerful incentive to recognize and tap into the talents of women.

Stage 4 organizations are proactive, and outside pressure is not the primary motivation to change. Stage 4 executives are convinced that valuing women is the right thing to do, both morally and for economic reasons, and they consider women true colleagues. What distinguishes Stage 4 from Stage 5 is the ongoing development and implementation of policies and practices linked to overall organizational change. In Stage 5 this is no longer required.

Stage 5: It's Part of Our Culture

Stage 5 represents the ideal organization. In this stage no group of employees feels disadvantaged, and valuing diversity permeates the organizational culture. These organizations are truly gender-blind because they have been gender-conscious. Employees are judged on their competence, not their gender. There is little sexual static, and the organization's mission and strategies reflect the concerns of women as well as men. In Stage 5 there is no need for specific management accountability on gender issues because women-friendly policies are firmly in place and widely accepted.

Admittedly, Stage 5 may seem unreachable. It may seem naive to believe that changes in the work environment can erase generations of stereotypes and prejudices against women. It may seem like wishful thinking to expect organizations to commit the resources needed to arrive at Stage 5. However, if it is true that fully utilizing women is an economic imperative, then moving into Stage 5 will eventually become a high priority for organizations that want to be competitive.

The Missing Link

As is clear from the preceding discussion, there is no quick organizational fix for moving from stage to stage. Organizations are pioneers each finding their own way over new terrain. However, my observation of organizations that are trying to do something about female underutilization is that most often they still don't see it as directly related to their restructuring efforts. They see what they call reengineering or reinventing as a top priority for the CEO and key executives because it is assumed to have a direct effect on the bottom line, but they relegate female underutilization to the human resources department because it hasn't historically been linked to profits.

I believe this is a mistake. In today's environment there is a strong connection between human resource utilization and reorganization. It can even be said that they are in a symbiotic relationship. For example, as organizations become more flexible in order to adapt to rapid change, they can provide opportunities for women who seek flexible work options. Many of the talents women bring to management—their comfort with sharing power and information, their ability to motivate in nontraditional ways, and their appar-

147

ent ease in responding to change—are crucial to organizations that are becoming less hierarchical and more weblike.

From both a strategic and financial point of view, structural reorganization should be undertaken in concert with efforts to rectify female underutilization. Flexibility and diversity are two keys to competitive advantage, and both are very closely related to the underutilization issue. There is no doubt in my mind that executives who recognize this relationship will find their change efforts more effective and their organizations more profitable.

Once they understand the relationship, many executives ask, "What do we do now, and how do we do it?" That question is addressed in the following chapter.

" AND FRANK, YOU'LL BE HERE, IN CHARGE OF
THINKING UP A BETTER ORGANIZATIONAL
ARRANGEMENT. "

"And Frank, you'll be here . . ." Tedd Goff Illustration, 1994 *Orange County Business Journal.*

9

The Process of Change

When an organization has identified the stage that best describes it, what next? It bears repeating that there is no quick fix for the underutilization problem. The only effective approach is to recognize that creating an environment where women are truly valued is an ongoing process closely related to the one required of organizations as they adapt over time to changes in the new global marketplace. There *are* solutions for specific gender problems like overt sexual harassment, pay inequity, and inflexible work arrangements, but while necessary, they are not sufficient to move an organization into Stage 5.

Raising awareness about the underutilization of women is similar to raising awareness about other cultural diversity issues or about the need to reengineer an organization. Top executives must understand why change is needed. If they don't, efforts to change the work environment will fail. That is why organizations committed to addressing gender issues must undertake the kind of gender awareness training that will be described in some detail later in this chapter.

For a variety of reasons, many executives don't think they need to be exposed to the kind of awareness training they support for others in their organizations. They may feel that their human resource people will keep them posted on how they should behave and that symbolic involvement on their part is enough. They may be concerned that participating in formal awareness training will require them to express emotions and attitudes they would rather keep private. Or they may worry that talking about how they feel will put them on the defensive and that they will be perceived as uncomfortable or confused.

However, many executives who have participated in awareness training have found it a positive experience. One such executive told me, "I finally understand why I question the competence of women. I never realized how I subconsciously see them as sex objects and how that has influenced the way I treat them." What made the training work for him, he said, was that the other men in the group felt the same way. Realizing that he was not alone made him feel less guilty. More important, the training helped him learn how to think differently about his interactions with his female colleagues.

Gender awareness training is often thought to be very confrontational, consisting of adversarial encounters and emotional outpourings. It need not be. If real organizational change is to occur, there has to be a candid discussion of values, feelings, biases, and unconscious behaviors. That means there will be some emotional tension and discomfort. However, with a qualified facilitator, awareness training is usually positive. A good facilitator channels discomfort so that it leads to behavioral change rather than feelings of guilt, as illustrated by the experience of executives of the Fortune 500 company discussed at the end of this chapter.

Some organizations are reluctant to provide employee awareness training because of the outcome of a class action suit in 1993. In that case, comments made by participants in a diversity workshop at Lucky Stores were used to support claims of discrimination.[1] Unfortunately for Lucky Stores, participants in the workshop were not advised that remarks made during the workshop could not be used against those who made them. For this kind of training to be successful, participants need to be candid. At the same time, ground rules need to be clearly articulated at the outset. When emotional issues surrounding gender surface in the process of changing an organization's culture, concern about lawsuits is understandable, and the Lucky Stores case has heightened this concern. However, competent facilitators and outside consultants can make sure that the problems faced by Lucky Stores are avoided.

Executives sometimes have a tendency to think that moving from one organizational stage to the next is so complicated that expert help is needed. This is not necessarily so. Often what's needed is simply expert thought about what *kind* of help to seek. In-house human resource people may know how to proceed. On the other hand, they may not, because many human resource people have never been trained in gender or diversity issues, much less management strategy. Historically their main responsibilities have been wages, benefits, labor relations, and specific labor complaints. In fact, one look at most textbooks used in personnel classes in business schools indicates that gender issues rarely made the index before 1992. Whether in-house people are capable by themselves of moving organizations from one stage to another depends on their knowledge and skills, and on the organization, the stage it is in, and the issues it faces.

Human resource people who have not been trained in cultural diversity issues such as gender have two options. They can learn about the issues by attending seminars, taking classes, or reading books. Or they can call on a consultant to help. The decision to use an outside consultant depends on a variety of factors. What is the organization's experience with consultants? Are there sufficient resources available to hire a consultant for other than superficial remedies? Will an outside consultant be able to deal with sensitive issues better than in-house personnel? In many cases, outside consultants are highly effective.

When an outside consultant works with top executives and human resource personnel, it is possible to build on the experience of other organizations, which saves time and dollars. Consultants often train in-house people, which is called "training the trainers," thus creating in-house expertise. Consultants can perform an objective assessment of the work environment because they are not part of the organization. They can act as a reliable sounding board for ideas because they have no investment in the status quo. Using consultants to address the underutilization of women in an organization is similar to using consultants to help re-engineer. Their main value is that they shorten the learning time for organizations facing new kinds of problems, and that they can more easily identify and champion what are often unpopular and painful change strategies.

The Change Cycle: Moving from Stage to Stage

When I speak to executives about gender issues, they express a similar range of concerns, regardless of what type of organization they lead: "We don't understand gender issues." "We don't know how to handle our ladies." "Our turnover is high, but we don't know why." "We feel we're being attacked by the women in our firm." "How do we make sure there is no sexual discrimination going on? What can we do?" Such comments exude a sense of frustration about how to proceed. Therefore, it is important to have a plan of action if an organization is to move from stage to stage.

Whether an outside consultant is used or not, there is a set of activities involved in moving organizations from one stage to another. These activities constitute what can be called a *cycle of change*.[2] As an organization moves from stage to stage, it consciously or subconsciously moves through this change cycle. Like the five organizational stages described in the previous chapter, the cycle of change is germane to both female underutilization and the reform of organizations so they become more flexible and effective. The cycle of change consists of:

- Assessing needs
- Increasing awareness and building skills
- Developing strategies and accountability
- Measuring and monitoring progress

Assessing Needs

Effective organizational change requires knowing how employees feel about their work environment, which is why the first part of the cycle involves a needs assessment. This knowledge can be generated in a variety of ways:

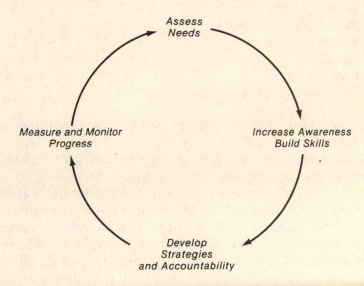

Change Cycle Necessary to Move from Stage to Stage.

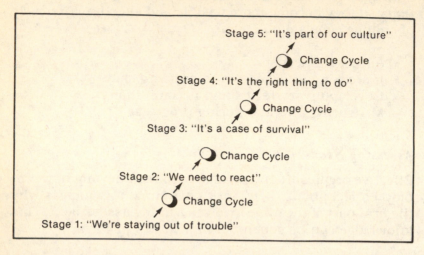

Stages of Awareness and Action.

- Surveys
- Executive interviews
- Focus groups
- Feedback to executives from surveys, interviews, and focus groups
- Forums and dialogue sessions

Needs assessment is well understood in most organizations, although it is often done in a superficial manner. A good in-depth assessment not only generates useful information, it also makes employees feel they are participating in the identification of changes that will ultimately affect them.

One way to assess how people feel about the environment in which they work is to ask them. *Surveys* can be done through questionnaires that ask employees to identify policies and practices that they think help or disadvantage them. It's important to understand that the way questions are phrased predetermines the kind of responses that are received. Therefore, special care needs to be taken in the formulation of questions, to ensure that they elicit the quality and quantity of information desired.

Another useful technique is to have an outside consultant conduct *executive interviews*. One-on-one interviews with key executives can yield data that might not be otherwise available, and they also tend to promote top-level involvement.

Focus groups are a commonly used marketing technique that elicit reactions from those who are considered a market for some product or service. Organizations today are using focus groups because employees are increasingly seen as consumers of managerial attention. Women, men, or employees who perform a specific function are brought together and asked to talk about topics such as communication problems, performance evaluations, or benefits. The purpose of the process is to learn how the participants feel about the organization's policies, procedures, or actions. Focus groups are usually small and characterized by an in-depth discussion of one or two topics. The expectation is that concrete recommendations will emerge from the discussion.

During the first part of the change cycle, executives need to receive *feedback from assessments* in the form of anonymous aggregate information obtained from interviews, surveys, and focus groups. Feedback ensures that executives understand how peers and subordinates perceive their current work environment. Many executives feel that employee perceptions do not reflect reality. The point of the assessment process is to impress on them that aggregate employee perceptions *constitute* the reality. After receiving feedback on an assessment of his firm, one midwestern mortgage banker said to me, "I see this as a journey . . . and it's not a short trip. When I saw the comments of a large number of women on paper, I began to realize that women in my organization don't feel understood or appreciated."

The banker's reaction is similar to that of other male executives when their organizations are assessed. It is often a revelation to them to learn how frustrated their female employees feel and how greatly the perceptions of men and women differ. They also begin to understand why it is easier to recruit women than to retain them. They see how career development programs, performance evaluation mechanisms, and informal networks favor men. They learn from the feedback that there is anxiety and fear not only among women but also among some men. For the first time, they may hear the term "fitting in" used in a negative way. Finally, the feedback process often conveys to executives that their organizations don't recognize or take stands on what women consider inappropriate behavior, and that some kind of forum for a nonthreatening dialogue between men and women is desperately needed.

What are *forums and dialogue sessions*, and how do they differ from focus groups? A forum is a place where dialogue can occur. In a forum there is no predetermined topic; the topics emerge from the discussion. The following example of a dialogue session run by an outside consultant illustrates how a good forum can work.[3]

Top male executives and female managers and professionals were invited to a corporate retreat, where they were divided into two groups and asked to make anonymous lists of questions and concerns they wanted to discuss with the other group. The men and the women met separately and wrote their questions on a flip chart. The two groups were then brought together in a process carefully facilitated by skilled outside male and female consultants. Each group was asked to identify the two major questions they wanted to discuss with the other group. The questions the men asked the women were:

1. What do you consider the ideal work environment for women?
2. What do you consider the foremost barrier that prevents women from advancing in this company?

The questions the women asked the men were:

1. We know you are uncomfortable with women in positions of power. What makes you so uncomfortable?
2. We know you think men and women are different. Why do you think that because we're different, we're not competent?

Notice the thrust of the questions. The men were asking, "*What's* the problem?" The women were asking, "*Why* the problem?" By using a dialogue session as a way to surface issues in an open forum, it was possible to identify differences in the way the men and women participants perceived gender issues. A forum like this one gives top executives an opportunity to analyze what was said and determine what needs to be done.

Increasing Awareness and Building Skills

The next phase of the change cycle involves increasing gender awareness and building skills. Real gender awareness usually requires specific awareness training. It is different from the gender awareness referred to earlier, in the discussion of the wake-up call. It entails an in-depth analysis of stereotypes, biases, communication styles, and so on, not merely a general recognition that there is a gender problem. The primary tools used to increase awareness and build skills are:

- Role playing
- Videos
- Case studies
- Skill development

Role playing is one good technique for increasing individual self-awareness of gender stereotypes and of the ways women are devalued. Role playing brings employees together to act out a situation in which stereotypes about women emerge. For example, a man may be asked to play the role of a woman who finds that she has not been invited to an all-male lunch after an important meeting, a lunch she knows will involve a follow-up discussion of the meeting. By playing the role of an excluded female colleague, the man experiences what she feels in a very direct way. These feelings are then discussed. Similarly, a woman may be asked to play the role of a man who has to choose between a male colleague and a female colleague for a major project that requires working together over a prolonged time. The goal of role playing is to walk a mile in someone else's shoes.

Another way to increase awareness is to use *videos* that depict men and women interacting in stereotypical ways. Today many companies produce videos on such subjects as sexual harassment, management style differences, mentoring, etc. An advantage of videos is that they depersonalize issues so that viewers feel free to talk about subjects that might otherwise make them uncomfortable. And because they are a form of entertainment, videos sometimes capture the interest of people who otherwise might not participate. The problem with most videos is that they tend to be somewhat stilted. On the other hand, it is possible to stop and start videos to emphasize specific issues.

The use of *case studies* can also foster gender awareness. Discussions of actual cases involving gender issues offer an opportunity for in-depth analysis of gender differences in a variety of contexts. Case studies take a good deal of time because participants need to read them thoroughly and think about them carefully if a useful discussion is to take place. However, the positive aspects of case studies are well known. They provide realistic examples that are much richer in detail than a video, and are more likely to elicit thoughtful and productive dialogue. Sometimes they generate helpful scenarios for alternative action.

Increasing awareness is only one part of this two-part

phase of the change cycle. It must be complemented by skill development. The building of skills that enable individuals to interact more effectively with those different from themselves takes place on two levels. Managers can develop their own interpersonal skills, such as the ability to listen, the ability to read nonverbal cues, the ability to conduct performance appraisals in culturally sensitive ways, and the ability to resolve intercultural conflict.[4] Managers also need to learn how to build multicultural teams.

The other level is skill development for employees. These may be technical skills, such as becoming computer literate, or they may be the more traditional language, math, and reasoning skills. In addition, it is important that managers encourage and make possible the development of interpersonal skills such as working as a team member and understanding cultural differences.

Developing Strategies and Accountability

Once an organizational assessment has been made, awareness has increased, and managerial as well as employee skills have been developed, it is time to work on strategies and managerial accountability. The development of an effective strategy to address the underutilization of women requires the participation of women, which can take many forms:

- Support groups
- Task forces
- Networks and councils

It also requires an organizational commitment to:

- Developing a change strategy
- Management accountability

There are many places in an organization where the concerns of women can be expressed and heard. In some firms women spontaneously start *support groups* to share information and help each other. These groups are most often informal and usually meet after work or at lunchtime. Over and over I hear stories of such groups forming when women meet by chance, find themselves sharing experiences, and then decide to get together on a regular basis.[5]

Pressure from support groups often leads to the creation of *networks and councils,* which have a more formal structure. The purpose of a woman's network or council is to provide managers with information about the group's concerns. Networks and councils may be composed of women from different units or geographical areas, or from one place or local unit. These groups are sanctioned by the corporation and usually meet in corporate facilities, perhaps during work hours. Councils and networks generally report to a CEO or diversity director, making suggestions and recommendations for change. Many organizations have similar networks and councils for other underrepresented groups as well.

Task forces are usually created by management for a specific purpose, such as investigating sexual harassment, identifying particular problems associated with gender (e.g., differential task assignments), or looking into issues like child care, flextime, or career development opportunities. A task force is usually expected to produce a report or issue a statement, after which it is disbanded. The value of a task force is that it symbolizes an organization's commitment to tackling a difficult problem. It can also be used to defuse an issue. Because task forces operate with clear boundaries for a set period of time, they are good mechanisms for producing specific recommendations.

Once it is clear what needs to be done, key executives begin *developing a change strategy*. This part of the cycle requires a choice of intervention activities. In Stages 4 and 5, the strategy and accountability phase must be clearly linked to performance evaluation, career training and development, succession planning, recruitment, and retention —in other words, to the organizational mission or business plan. A crucial part of this phase is the examination and evaluation of systems, policies, and practices to identify those that disadvantage women or result in their underutilization.

This is perhaps the most difficult yet most important part of any real change strategy. It is an activity male executives often find hard to grasp. For example, men rarely realize that meeting times and mandated after-hours socializing disadvantage women, who often have family responsibilities that make it difficult for them to meet late in the afternoon or at breakfast time, or to devote hours to golf or drinking after work. Practices like this are hard to identify because they're so ingrained, but they must be changed because they contribute to the devaluation and underutilization of women.

In addition to overhauling policies and practices, strong *management accountability* measures are needed if change is to occur. Accountability can be instituted in a number of ways. Managers can be evaluated on whether the climate in their units improves according to a set of predetermined criteria. Pay and bonuses can be tied to the achievement of change goals. Managers can be assessed on how they are evaluated by the women with whom they work. Without accountability measures, the probability of real change is minimal. Rewards and punishments are still the best way to change behavior, so if there are no rewards or punishments linked to change, it probably won't take place.

Measuring and Monitoring Progress

To ascertain the effectiveness of awareness training, skill development, and other interventions, they have to be measured and monitored. Otherwise it is impossible to know whether the benefits of a given intervention are greater than its costs. The primary techniques of measuring and monitoring are:

- Monitoring recruitment, turnover, absenteeism
- Pre- and post-intervention interviews
- Estimating the costs and benefits of change efforts

While it is relatively simple to quantify recruitment, turnover, and absenteeism, it is more difficult to determine the costs and benefits of specific interventions. However, unless there is a way to measure the costs and benefits of any investment in change, top executives will not support change efforts. The fuller utilization of women has to be linked to the bottom line, and that means generating numbers to justify the easy-to-calculate costs of training and skill development.

Monitoring recruitment, turnover, and absenteeism means keeping track of how many women have been recruited over specific time intervals, how many leave, and how many days a year women are absent from work relative to men. Most organizations monitor their male and female employees in some manner. It has been high female turnover and absenteeism that has made organizations ask questions about their traditional culture. Large CPA and law firms, in particular, have discovered that they are losing potential female partners, and they know they can no longer attribute this phenomenon to work/family conflicts alone. For example, in 1993 Deloitte & Touche launched a major training program in an effort to address their turnover problem.[6]

In addition to numbers, it is important to ask the people who are the target of change efforts whether they feel the efforts have been beneficial. That is, do they feel more productive, more valued, and more effective as a result of training or skill development? At the same time, it is important to make sure that expectations about change efforts are the same for everyone—key executives, those participating in the efforts, and those implementing them.

The best way to obtain a consensus on the goals and expected outcomes of any activity is to conduct *pre- and post-intervention interviews*—that is, to ask all the participants about their perceptions of those goals and outcomes before and after the activity.[7] The "before" answers can then be used as a standard by which to measure whether expectations have been met.

It is essential that pre-activity expectations are consistent for all interested parties, because if there is disagreement at the outset as to what the change effort is to accomplish, it will be difficult to come to agreement about its value after it has been completed. If interviews reveal that expectations vary widely, it may be necessary to rethink the activity so that everyone concerned shares similar expectations.

Before-and-after interviews and questionnaires, while they may not generate hard numbers, do provide a reading of the qualitative context in which change efforts take place. Unless those targeted for change feel that training or skill development helps them, recruitment, turnover, and absenteeism numbers are unlikely to change. More important, the interview and questionnaire data can be used as an indicator of the effectiveness of those responsible for the intervention. It may be that the goals of a change effort are valid but those implementing it are not doing a good job. Well-structured surveys and interviews can help organizations assess the worth of a change effort and the way it is being conducted.

Once individual and organizational expectations about the goals of change efforts are clear, before-and-after data on recruitment, turnover, and absenteeism make it possible to begin *estimating the costs and benefits of change efforts.* If recruitment improves, turnover goes down, and absenteeism decreases after awareness training and skill building, there's a good chance that the interventions are working. It is not always possible to show a direct causal relationship between the numbers and change efforts, since other factors are always operating simultaneously. However, this should in no way deter organizations from monitoring their progress.

Estimating the costs and benefits of change efforts is additionally complicated because the costs are usually easier to quantify than the benefits. We know how to measure the cost of hiring a consultant, or the cost of a trainer's time or of materials or of employee time spent in training. But how do we measure an increase in a potential manager's feeling of self-worth? How do we measure an increase in technology literacy or a better understanding of gender differences? Any of these changes may make a woman more productive or more credible in the eyes of her male peers, but how do we affix numbers to them? Any of these changes may enhance a woman's morale and prompt her to reconsider leaving a company, but how do we measure that? Only with great difficulty. That's why it's important to combine survey and interview data with monitoring. If a change activity helps create a climate more hospitable to women, it can be assumed that recruitment will be easier, turnover will drop, and absenteeism will decrease. Then the costs of change activities will seem warranted.

If it is a challenge to come up with numbers that can be used to estimate the costs of addressing female underutilization, it is even more difficult to calculate the costs of *not* paying attention to these issues. Some academics suggest that the cost of turnover among female managers needs to be looked at in a human capital framework.[8] For example, it has been estimated that in large companies the cost of losing, recruiting, and retraining one professional woman can range from $30,000 to $50,000. This is what is meant by human capital costs, which include severance packages, recruitment advertising, candidate travel payments, interview time, and search firm fees. Because of human capital costs, many companies today are beginning to see the economic sense of investing in change efforts that make it easier to retain women.

There is one other factor that makes estimating the costs and benefits of change efforts, difficult: the time span in which results are expected. If key executives think they can immediately reduce their recruiting, turnover, and absenteeism costs by instituting training and skill development, they will be disappointed. Real change takes time. Training and skill development, whether aimed at women or at men who need to understand how to work better with women, aren't effective over a short period of time. They require an ongoing commitment, and their benefits cannot be seen immediately. For this reason, while costs may be easy to identify and estimate in the short run, the larger benefits need to be estimated in the long run. However, the mere existence of programs to change the work environment will have positive effects on women employees. Placing a dollar figure on these effects remains a challenge for academics and human resource specialists.

The Change Cycle, Best Practices, and One Fortune 500 Company

Because addressing female underutilization issues is relatively new, there is a search for what has been termed "best practices." This term means policies and practices—intervention activities—that are considered the best in improving productivity and profits. At the first Conference on the Workforce of the Future, convened by Secretary of Labor Robert Reich and Secretary of Commerce Ronald Brown in July 1993, the president of a large pension fund, after hearing about the best practices of a number of companies, said, "Fund managers will be hesitant to invest in firms which merely allege to use their human resources wisely." His message was that there needs to be evidence of a causal relationship between change efforts and productivity. Significantly, some evidence is emerging. A study by Covenant Investment Management reported in 1993 that companies with strong EEO compliance outperformed the Standard & Poor's 500 stock market average by 2.4 percent a year over the previous five years, while companies with poor EEO records underperformed by 8 percent a year over the same period.[9]

Just as there is no one best model, there is no such thing as one set of best practices. Each organization has to analyze its own problems and design programs best suited to its particular situation. As Louis Gerstner, currently CEO of IBM, said while he was CEO of RJR Nabisco, "There are no prizes for predicting rain. There are only prizes for building arks."[10] Nonetheless, as an organization formulates strategies, it is useful to learn about what other organizations and government agencies are doing. For this reason, and because of its innovative nature, I want to describe an effort that enabled one Fortune 500 company to move from one organizational stage to another.

The assessment and tracking of career-oriented women in a particular unit of this Fortune 500 company started in earnest in 1990. A focus on diversity, especially the utilization and retention of women and minorities, had been part of the organization's business strategy since 1988. The concern about women surfaced, in part, because of a higher than normal turnover rate of female managers.

The company had an eighteen-member Leadership Team made up of key policymakers, four of whom were women. Concerned about the high turnover, the Leadership Team chartered a Task Force composed of ten of the company's senior women managers to get at the roots of the problem. The Task Force, using what is called a "Total Quality" process, spent many hours defining what they saw as their "current reality" and what they saw as a possible "future reality." The outcome of their effort is informative.

The Task Force created two very comprehensive and complex flow charts describing the two realities. The current reality chart contained approximately fifty boxes with arrows connecting one to another. The boxes contained statements such as "White males control the power base and value system," with an arrow pointing to "Policies, practices and benefits are determined by men." A box with "Men and women communicate differently" had an arrow leading to a box that said, "Women are often not heard and/or understood." Another box noted, "Some women are frustrated and/or angry," with an arrow pointing to "Some women behave in ways that adversely affect their performance," which in turn led to "Career is slowed and/or stopped." Still another box said, "Women assume that assignment planning and promotions are different for men and women," with an arrow to "Women assume decisions reflect institutionalized sexism," which led to "Women don't perceive they can have a career at the company." There were also a number of boxes that had to do with balancing work and family, such as "In society, family needs are generally considered a woman's responsibility," which pointed to "Personnel policies and benefits, as written and administered, may not be sufficient to meet a woman's unique needs," with an arrow to "Some women are tired and dissatisfied with trying to balance work and family." This box led to "Some women are leaving the company." The overall message was clearly that the current reality—the lack of a share in the power base, coupled with the work environment—caused some women to leave.

The future reality chart had fewer boxes. Here the boxes showed that by making the work environment more inclusive of women, "the organization wins." The boxes on this chart contained statements such as "Men and women work hard to hear and understand each other," with an arrow to "People spend less time and energy on non-value-added activities at work," implying that they are more productive. "The power base and value system is shared by men and women and reflects diverse styles" had an arrow to "Policies and benefits meet diverse needs." All of these boxes led straight to "Women have a more acceptable work/life balance," "Fewer women leave the company," and ultimately,

"The company wins!" The future reality chart included other boxes leading to these same "fewer women leave" and "company wins" boxes.

The Task Force decided to use outside consultants to help them communicate the implications of their research to the Leadership Council. The consultants suggested that the women do some exercises to further establish how they felt about themselves and their work environment, and also that they analyze what they learned from developing the charts. After doing this, the Task Force members were convinced that they needed to convert their complex charts into one simple message. The consultants facilitated their framing of the message, but the Task Force members themselves decided how to do it. As it turned out, the way their observations were communicated to the Leadership Team constituted a message in itself.

The Leadership Team was invited to sit in front of a stage upon which all the Task Force members were seated. Three of the women on the Task Force sat at the edge of the stage and acted as a Greek chorus. A female unit manager was the first to speak. She made a statement taken from one of the original boxes on the current reality chart. She said, "Personnel policies and benefits as written and administered are not sufficient to meet the needs of women employees." After she finished, the chorus chanted, "Men control the power base and the value system. Men and women communicate differently. Because men control the power base and value system, and because men and women communicate differently, often I am not heard or understood." At this point the female unit manager quietly walked off the stage. She was followed by another Task Force member, who said, "When I try to emulate male behavior, I suppress my true self." The chorus then repeated the refrain, and the second woman quietly walked off the stage. This continued until all the statements in the boxes had been expressed and all the women had disappeared. The message was obvious. Given the current reality, women will leave the company! The female unit manager said that one of the men on the Leadership Team later told her, "I knew what you were doing, and I wanted to get up and stop you from leaving."

The dramatization had a profound impact on the male executives. When all the women were gone, the men were left perplexed. The consultants then used an interactive exercise called the "Fishbowl Technique" to analyze the dramatization's effect. The men sat in a circle facing each other, surrounded by the women, who returned and sat in an outer circle. The men were asked to discuss with each other, aloud, what they heard during the dramatization and how they felt about what they heard. The women sat quietly and listened. The men made comments like these: "Ours is a male-dominated company." "The women feel we don't listen to them." "Women think they have to act like men to get ahead." "The women feel the organization is inflexible and not sympathetic to the needs of those with family responsibilities." Many of the men also shared their own work and family experiences and the emotions involved.

After hearing how the men felt about the message conveyed in the drama, the women moved into the inside circle, the "fishbowl," surrounded by the men. The women then talked about their reactions to the male comments. In essence, the women said: "The rules are changing and men are not sure how to act," "Men fear reverse discrimination," and "It is difficult for men to express their feelings." They also sensed that the men didn't really understand why the women felt as they did about their work environment. The Fishbowl Technique was also used to facilitate discussion about the comments made on the future reality chart.

The Task Force dramatization provoked a great deal of interest in gender issues and raised awareness. As a result of the dramatization and the feedback process, the Leadership Team decided to sit down with the Task Force, review its specific recommendations, and develop action plans based on what they learned. This was the beginning of a genuine shared organizational vision that reflected the concerns of the unit's men and women and its key executives. It was a major step toward the decrease in female turnover. Not only was gender awareness raised, but there was a honing of male and female communication skills. Men and women listened to each other more acutely and were better able to articulate their feelings and emotions. The effort was successful because the Leadership Team believed in the importance of retaining and effectively utilizing women as a competitive business advantage.

Because of what happened in this unit, there has been a shared interest in generating change in other parts of the Fortune 500 company. This example, while unique in many ways, illustrates an effort to move from Stage 2 (We Need to React) toward Stage 4 (It's the Right Thing to Do). It shows how one unit of a large organization went through the change cycle in an effort to address the underutilization issue. It shows an organization on the move to leverage the talents of its professional women.

Understanding the five organizational stages, the cycle of change necessary to move from one to another, and the relationship of the stages to better human resource utilization and organizational reform is critical to economic competitiveness. Are other countries aware of this relationship? Do they know that women are an underutilized resource? These questions are discussed in the following chapter.

10

Female Underutilization Worldwide

In 1993 Deloitte & Touche, a large accounting firm, placed a full two-page ad in the *Wall Street Journal*. Most of the space was filled with these words written in large letters: LAWSUITS, TAXES, WOMEN IN THE WORKPLACE, RUNAWAY HEALTH COSTS, TQM, AND GLOBAL COMPETITION. Underneath, in smaller letters, the words and phrases were translated into challenges aimed at executives. One of them read, "You are concerned about how leadership potential is wasted when women aren't given the chance to take on top corporate roles."[1] Although the ad did not explicitly link the various concerns it identified, the implication was clear: women in the workplace are an important factor in making organizations more globally competitive.

In other countries the relationship between the underutilization of women and global competitiveness is also becoming clear. One look at what is happening in Japan, Britain, and the countries of the European Union (EU) tells the story.[2] Countries such as Taiwan, China, Singapore, and some Latin American nations are also current or potential competitors of the United States, but I exclude them here because of the difficulty of obtaining reliable data.[3]

Comparative Underutilization Measures

National political and business leaders increasingly suggest that the role of women cannot be ignored given changing demographics and the need to use all human resources effectively. Their words are often more visible than their deeds. Still, efforts are being made, some symbolic and some substantive, to underscore the importance of female underutilization. For example, in December 1992 a conference called Equal to the Task was convened to mark Britain's presidency of the European Council, a deliberative body of the European Union. The purpose of the conference was to give major EU government and corporate employers an opportunity to talk about diversity, particularly the need to provide equal opportunities for working women. Agnes Hubert, head of the Equal Opportunities Unit of the European Commission, noted at the conference that 52 percent of the EU population and 40 percent of its labor market are women, and that promoting equal opportunities for women in EU countries is an economic issue, not a women's issue.[4]

President Clinton, visiting Japan's Waseda University in July 1993, told a thousand students that "Japan with its low birthrate and its long life expectancy will have to take advantage of the skills of women if it wants to continue to grow economically."[5] His comment, and the fact that it was made in Japan, illustrates a growing awareness that women should be viewed in economic terms.

In the United States, the Glass Ceiling Commission was created as part of the Civil Rights Act of 1991. Chaired by the secretary of labor, it is composed of twenty-one members representing business, labor, education, and government. The commission's purpose is to study and monitor corporations and government agencies to make sure that barriers to the advancement of women are removed. The commission has conducted hearings around the country in an attempt to learn where barriers exist and how or if organizations are dislodging them. Based on testimony given at these hearings and research findings from studies funded by the commission, a set of recommendations will be prepared and sent to the president in late 1995. According to a report released by the commission in March 1995, women in the United States have moved from the clerical basement to the managerial mezzanine, but the door to the executive suite still remains largely closed. In 1993 92.5 percent of successful women executives surveyed by Korn Ferry said they believed a "glass ceiling still exists"; two years later, in the words of the *Los Angeles Times*, the glass ceiling seemed "more like a steel cage."[6] It seems safe to predict that by the end of 1995 men will continue to have access to organizational elevators while most women are forced to take the stairs.

In the EU countries as well, women are still climbing the stairs and not being shown the elevator. However, in 1992 eleven EU states (excluding Britain) signed a protocol stating that by majority vote the members could act to ensure equality between men and women at work. And a 1992 EU document, "The Position of Women in the Labor Market," suggested that "throughout Europe women are gearing up under the sign of discrimination."[7]

In Britain, too, women rarely ride an elevator. In 1990 the Hansard Society, whose aim is to encourage citizen understanding of and participation in parliamentary government, published a report much like the one the U.S. Glass Ceiling Commission produced. The Hansard report documented pervasive barriers to the appointment of women to senior professional positions, outmoded attitudes about women, and direct and indirect discrimination.[8] That report was a forerunner of the important efforts now underway in the National Health Service, as discussed below.

In Japan women generally remain in the clerical basement, although a few have reached the first floor. It can be said that Japanese women are just learning that elevators exist. Yet there are indications of a growing awareness in Japan that women constitute an economic resource. Because of a labor shortage of professionals, the beginning of a women's movement, and the opening of doors to traditionally male professions, Japan in the next few decades could experience an influx of women into its workforce much like what happened in the 1970s and 1980s in the United States. If it does, Japan could become an even more formidable competitor for the United States than it is today.

Global economic conditions in the early 1990s were such that tapping the talents of women (as well as men) took a back seat to the creation of jobs. However, as conditions improve, the demand for skilled labor and potential leaders will increase. Countries that recognize the value of women as an economic resource today will be the best prepared to compete internationally tomorrow, for everywhere in the world there is a limited pool of potential managers.

Comparing the underutilization of women in Japan, Britain, and the EU countries is difficult because every country collects, categorizes, and reports information differently. However, it is possible to give a thumbnail sketch by comparing available data. That is the intent of Table 1.

Table 1 shows that the United States produces more educated women, has a higher female labor participation rate, has more women in traditionally male occupations, and has more women in middle and upper management positions than do the other countries. The large number of women receiving M.D.'s, M.B.A.'s, Ph.D.'s, and law degrees (in addition to bachelor's degrees in all fields) attests to the large supply of potential professional women in the United States. The EU countries also have high percentages of women in professional schools, although their absolute numbers are few in comparison to U.S. numbers. The fact that only 14 percent of the Japanese women who go to college attend four-year schools and that only 26 percent of all Japanese university students are women seems surprising, because most Japanese children graduate from high school. However, for Japanese women a four-year college degree primarily means a better chance for a "good" husband, not a good job. In Japan a college degree from a leading university helps men but not women obtain career positions. Even with a degree from a leading university, a woman is rarely hired for a career position. Thus, there has historically been little incentive for women to get degrees from major universities. This is changing, albeit slowly.

Table 1 provides a very general comparison of the various countries in the context of the underutilization measures discussed in Chapter 3. Clearly, the table is no more than a snapshot at a given time. What it does show is that women are underutilized around the world. However, in the United States there are more women than elsewhere poised to assume leadership positions.

Comparative Support Mechanisms

The underutilization measures in Table 1 tell only part of the story. For a better comparison of U.S. women with those in competing countries, it is also necessary to assess the quality of the environment in which they work. The presence or absence of laws and support systems says much about the future of women. Table 2 compares countries in the context of laws and other types of support mechanisms that help women take advantage of career opportunities.

As Table 2 shows, the United States has in place many more support systems than most of its economic competitors. Discrimination and equal opportunity laws in the United States carry sanctions for noncompliance, and there are many women's networks and professional organizations. Women have considerable access to male-dominated profes-

Table 1. Comparative Underutilization of Women

	United States	Japan	Britain	EU Countries
Labor participation rates	Women constitute 56% of the labor force. Labor participation rate starts at age 18 and peaks at 45, with only a slight decrease of 2% during childbearing years (33–35). 52% who work have children under the age of six. Female participation rate projections for the year 2000 are ~ 62%.[1]	Women constitute 40% of the labor force. 50% of women work. The average length of continuous employment is 7.2 years. Participation rate starts at 18 and peaks before 20. It drops dramatically 23% from ages 20–24, increases slowly again until ages 35–40, but never returns to the original rate.[2]	60% of women work, and comprise 44% of the total work force.[3] Labor participation rate starts at 18 and rises to one peak at ages 20–24. Drops 8% at 25–34 and increases again to its highest peak at 35–39.[4]	41.2% of the labor force is women.[5] 50% of all EU women work. 16% of women with children under 6 are employed. Labor participation rate starts at 18, peaks before childbearing years (25–29), and decreases from then on.[4]
Unemployment and underemployment	The overall unemployment rate for women is 5.3% vs. 5.1% for men. 17% of the labor force works part-time. 68% of part-time workers are women.[6] 27% of employed women work part-time.[1]	The overall unemployment rate for men and women is the same— 2.3%.[6] 18% of the labor force works part-time.[2] 70% of part-time workers are women.[9] 27% of employed women work part-time.[2]	The overall unemployment rate for women is 7% vs. 9% for men.[7] 22% of the labor force works part-time.[5] 90% of part-time workers are women.[3] 45% of employed women work part-time.[5]	The overall unemployment rate for women is 14% vs. 7% for men.[8] 13% of the labor force works part-time.[6] ~ 80% of part-time workers are women.[1] 12% of employed women work part-time.[5]

Underrepresentation (% managerial)[10]	Sex-segregated occupations	Pay equity
In large organizations 41% of middle managers are women. 3%–5% are top executives.[11]	High percentage of women in traditionally male occupations and professions. Males advance faster than females in female-dominated areas (e.g., nursing).[16]	Women earn 70% of men's wages.[21] Parity is closer for blue-collar than for white-collar workers.[22]
In large organizations 6% of middle managers are women.[12] Less than 1% are top executives.[13]	In all industries at all levels, except community service, women have less than 10% representation.[6] 99% of clerical jobs are held by women.[17] 98% of career-track workers are men.[18]	Women earn 50% of men's wages.[23]
In large organizations women comprise 29% of middle managers.[14] 3% are top executives.[3]	42% of women are employed in service organizations.[19] 50% of female managers are in office work, catering, and retail.[20]	Women earn 70% of men's earnings.[6] This gap is believed to be wider than in any other EU country.[24]
In large organizations women comprise 18% of middle managers. 1.5% are top executives.[15]	Very little data available, except that there is no representation of women exceeding 26% in managerial positions by occupation.[6]	Women earn 85% of men's earnings.[6]

(continued)

Table 1. (Continued)

	United States	Japan	Britain	EU Countries
Education	52% of college students are women. Women represent 30% of medical students, 30%–40% of M.B.A. students, 40% of law students, 15% of engineering students.[25]	26% of college students are women. 14% of women attend a four-year-school.[23] Most attend a two-year or junior college. 5% of law students are women. 20% of humanities students are women. There are no business schools in Japan.[26]	50% of the college and university population is women.[27] 50% of law and medical students are women.[28]	48% of college students are women. 40% of business, economics, and law graduates are female.[29]

Source: Compiled by Kim Jaussi, 1993.
1. Marianne A. Ferber and Brigid O'Farrell, eds., *Work and Family* (Washington, D.C.: National Academy Press, 1991).
2. Jyosei Shokugo Zaidan, "Female Employment Organization," *Working Women Encyclopedia* (Tokyo: Toyo Keizai Shinposha, 1991).
3. Clare Bebbington, "Ladies Don't Climb Ladders," *Eurobusiness,* December 1988, 12–17.
4. ILO, *Yearbook of Labor Statistics,* 1992.
5. Marilyn J. Davidson and Cary L. Cooper, eds., *European Women in Business and Management* (London: Paul Chapman, 1993).
6. "Working Women of the World," compilation of graphs by one of the author's students, 1992.
7. "Women and the Labour Market: Result from 1991 Labour Force Survey," *Employment Gazette,* September 1992, 433.
8. Commission of the European Communities, *Social Europe,* March 1991, 26.
9. James Steingold, "A Feminist Politician in Tokyo Uses Anger and Pranks to Battle Despair," *New York Times,* March 14, 1993.
10. "Managerial" is used here in a very general way to describe positions in middle to upper management. The term "manager" is often vague and can include administrative work as well, but not the top executive level. "Top executives" are those with primary budget and decision-making authority.
11. Korn Ferry International with the UCLA Anderson Graduate School of Management, *Decade of the Executive Woman,* 1993.

178

12. "It's Not the Kind of Job I'd Line Up For," *Newsweek*, May 24, 1993, 33–37.

13. "Japan Inc.: Peeking Inside the Closed Corporation," *Working Woman*, June 1992, 20.

14. Val Hammond, "Opportunity 2000: A Cultural Change Approach to Equal Opportunity," *Women in Management Review* 7, no. 7 (1992): 3–10.

15. Ariane Berthoin Antal and Camilla Krebsbach-Gnath, "Women in Management: Unused Resources in the Federal Republic of Germany," in Nancy J. Adler and Dafna N. Izraeli, eds., *Women in Management Worldwide* (Armonk, N.Y.: M. E. Sharpe, 1988).

16. Myra H. Strober, "Gender and Occupational Segregation," *International Encyclopedia of Education*, 2d ed. (Oxford, England: Pergamon Press, 1994).

17. Anne B. Fisher, "Japanese Working Women Strike Back," *Fortune*, May 31, 1993, 22.

18. Teresa Watanabe, "Japan Inc.: No Friend to Women," *Los Angeles Times*, September 19, 1992.

19. Beverly Alimo-Metcalfe, "What a Waste! Women in the National Health Service," *Women in Management Review and Abstracts* 6, no. 5 (1991): 17–24.

20. Beverly Alimo-Metcalfe and Colleen Wedderburn-Tate, "The United Kingdom," in Davidson and Cooper, *European Women*, 16–42.

21. This aggregate figure from the *Wall Street Journal* (see n. 22) includes all occupations and levels and may not accurately reflect pay differences in specific occupations and/or levels.

22. "Three Decades after the Equal Pay Act, Women's Wages Remain Far from Parity," *Wall Street Journal*, B-1, B-10.

23. Kazuko Watanabe, "The Cold War with Japan: How Are Women Paying for It?" *Ms.*, November–December 1991, 18–22.

24. "Extent of Discrimination against Women in Employment in the U.K.," Institute of Management Foundation, Corby, England, 1992.

25. *Statistical Abstract of the United States*, 1993.

26. Mary C. Brinton, *Women and the Economic Miracle* (Berkeley: University of California Press, 1993), 203.

27. Elaine Mitchell Attais, journalist, conversation with author, Beverly Hills, California, May 24, 1993.

28. Barbara Mills, "Equal Opportunities—Policy into Practice," speech delivered at the Equal to the Task conference, Birmingham, England, December 7, 1992.

29. *Education in OECD Countries, 1987–88*, special ed. (Paris: Organization for Economic Cooperation and Development, 1990).

Table 2. Comparative Support Mechanisms

	United States	Japan	Britain	EU Countries
Equal employment opportunity/pay laws	Title VII of the Civil Rights Act of 1964. Equal Employment Opportunities Commission (EEOC) given power to enforce Title VII in 1972 under Equal Employment Opportunities Act. Equal Pay Act of 1963.	Equal Employment Opportunity Law (EEOL) enacted in 1986. No sanctions.	Sex Discrimination Act of 1975. Equal Pay Act of 1970. Employment Act of 1989.	Article 119 of Treaty of Rome. 1963. EU directives on equal opportunities. Equal pay and equal opportunities laws in many EU countries.
Government and/or corporate initiatives	Federal Commission on the Glass Ceiling, established by the U.S. Department of Labor.[1] State and local commissions on the status of women. Large number of corporate and government programs aimed at recruiting and retaining women.	No widespread government or corporate initiatives.	Equal Opportunities Commission. Opportunity 2000. New Horizons for Women regional campaigns.[2] Women's Unit in National Health Service.	EU directives on equal treatment, equal pay, and social protections including burden of proof, parental leave, occupational and statutory social protection, and protection for women who are pregnant or have recently given birth.[3] New Opportunities for Women (NOW) initiative.[4]

Work/family support	1993 Family Leave Act, 12 weeks unpaid leave, with job security. Many corporate and government flexible work hours, job-sharing programs.	Law enacted in April 1992 granting up to one year's childcare leave for both parents.[5]	18-week paid maternity leave for full-time employees who have worked for two years and another 11-week unpaid leave with the right to return to work.[6]	EU Commission's Recommendation for Childcare mandated Family Leave Acts in most EU countries. Flexible work hours and job-sharing programs increasing.[3]
Women's movement/networks	Many established women's networks, e.g., National Organization for Women, National Women's Political Caucus, Business and Professional Women. Many professional women's groups. 30-year-old national women's movement.	A few women's organizations, e.g., Japan Pacific Resource Network (JPRN), Asian Women's Association.[7] No major women's movement.[8]	Growing number of women's organizations, e.g., Women in Management, Women in Banking. Various professional women's groups. Emerging and rapidly growing women's movement.[9]	Indications of a women's movement. Established professional women's network: European Women's Management Development (EWMD).[6] Growing number of women's organizations, e.g., Association of Working Women, Women in Business (WIB) in Germany, and the Frankfurt Forum (a network of foreign and German women managers).[10]

(continued)

Table 2. (Continued)

	United States	Japan	Britain	EU Countries
Differences in career path training	Relatively easy for women to enter traditionally male professions. Multiple types of training available for women. Impediments for women at upper-middle management level. Many women starting firms.[11]	Companies do not track men and women equally and do not offer equal opportunities to women. Men trained throughout the corporation as generalist, women as clerical. Many female-owned and female-run small businesses.[12]	Many training programs for men and women, but men and women trained differently. Abundance of training at the skill level and divergence at the upper management level. Men have more access to broader management development programs than women. 25% of the self-employed are women.[13]	In-house training programs that filter out women.[10] Because of denied access to training, women are promoted less often than men. In Germany, apprenticeship practices disadvantage women.[14] Many women starting firms.[14]

Source: Compiled by Kim Jaussi, 1993.
1. See "Committee Seeks to Define Glass Ceiling," *USA Today*, December 9, 1992, 9B.
2. "Equal to the Task," EDG U.K. fact sheet, 6–12.
3. Commission of the European Communities, *Social Europe*, March 1991.
4. Commission of the European Communities, *Equal Opportunities for Women and Men*, March 1991, 7.
5. "Men Take Advantage of Child-Care Leave," *Nikkei Weekly*, February 15, 1993.

6. Valerie Hammond, "Women in Management in Great Britain," in Nancy J. Adler and Dafna N. Izraeli, eds., *Women in Management Worldwide* (Armonk, N.Y.: M. E. Sharpe, 1988), 168–86.

7. Kazuko Watanabe, "The Cold War With Japan: How Are Women Paying for It?" *Ms.*, November–December 1991, 18–22.

8. Sumiko Iwao, *The Japanese Woman* (New York: Free Press, 1993).

9. Valerie Hammond and Viki Holton, "Great Britain: The Scenario for Woman Managers in Britain in the 1990s," in Nancy J. Adler and Dafna N. Izraeli, eds., *Competitive Frontiers* (Cambridge, Mass.: Blackwell, 1994), 224–42.

10. Ariane Berthoin Antal and Camilla Krebsbach-Gnath, "Women in Management: Unused Resources in the Federal Republic of Germany," in Adler and Izraeli, *Women in Management Worldwide*.

11. Joline Godfrey, *Our Wildest Dreams* (New York: HarperBusiness, 1992).

12. Mary C. Brinton, *Women and the Economic Miracle* (Berkeley: University of California Press, 1993), 32–33.

13. Beverly Alimo-Metcalfe and Colleen Wedderburn-Tate, "The United Kingdom," in Marilyn J. Davidson and Cary Cooper, eds., *European Women in Business and Management* (London: Paul Chapman, 1993), 16–42.

14. Ariane Berthoin Antal and Dafna N. Izraeli, "A Global Comparison of Women in Management," in Ellen A. Fagenson, ed., *Women in Management* (Newbury Park, Calif.: Sage, 1993), 68.

183

sions and occupations, and there is a strong women's movement. This is not so in Japan, where laws have no teeth and there are few women's organizations and a weak national women's movement. Most important, access to male-dominated professions is limited in Japan. In Britain there are laws with sanctions, and major corporate and government initiatives. There is a growing number of women's organizations, as well as a women's movement that is gaining strength. However, men and women are prepared differently for careers, and women do not have as much access to managerial and executive training as men do.

The EU countries today are aware of the underutilization issue as a result of the Directives of the Commission of the European Communities, which are discussed below. These directives mandate changes that will eventually facilitate the advancement of all women. A strong EU professional network is in place, and a growing number of profession-specific organizations are forming. However, women receive relatively little support when it comes to training and career development. In 1990, recognizing this deficiency, the Commission of the European Communities launched an initiative called New Opportunities for Women (NOW) to promote the training of women and address the difficulties they encounter specifically because they are women.[9] Traditional apprenticeship practices in many European countries disadvantage women because they were developed for men. However, women have begun to enter male-dominated professions, and it can be anticipated that this will continue.

Overall, the United States has a better support system for women than its competitors. Women have better access to all professions and managerial positions. They have many strong professional women's organizations. And they benefit from a thirty-year-old national women's movement. The U.S. advantage can be seen more clearly if we take a closer look at support mechanisms in the EU countries, Britain, and Japan.

The European Union

The EU has launched a major campaign to provide opportunities for women to utilize their education and talents more fully. Part of this campaign was the Equal to the Task conference mentioned earlier. Such a conference would not have been possible even a decade ago. To judge from the conference participation of the EU member countries, it is clear that the issue of women as an economic resource is on the minds of European corporate and government leaders.

Because of their size, individual European countries do not constitute a serious challenge to America's economic well-being, but in the aggregate they do. Christine Crawley, a member of the European Parliament, notes that women in the European Union "still have a long way to go before they catch up with men—economically, politically and socially."[10] It follows that they also have a long way to go before they catch up with the United States. However, Crawley and others who are trying to improve working conditions for women point out that the Committee on Women's Rights of the European Parliament, together with the Commission of the European Communities, is providing a legal and programmatic framework that will assist governments and corporations in efforts to enhance the role of women in the labor force.

One of the major objectives of the European Union is to improve living and working conditions for the people of Europe. The main problem facing women in the EU, as in other countries, is inequality at work. To address this and similar problems, the EU has adopted five directives that are worth noting, for the member nations have agreed to abide by them, and so they portend changes in EU organizations.[11] The directives mandate:

- Legal guarantees enforcing equal pay for work of equal value
- Equal treatment with regard to recruitment, vocational training, and promotion

- Equal treatment in social security matters, with the goal of achieving equal treatment in statutory social security schemes
- Equal treatment in occupational social security schemes
- Equal treatment in self-employment, including those employed in agriculture[12]

The United Kingdom and Opportunity 2000

An example of how the EU directives can translate into an individual government initiative is the Opportunity 2000 effort launched in the United Kingdom in October 1991.[13] Opportunity 2000 is a public/private initiative designed to increase the quantity and quality of women's participation in the workforce. It grew out of the work of a team of women led by Lady Howe, chair of Business in the Community, a foundation supported by nearly five thousand major U.K. companies, along with representatives of government, trade unions, and the voluntary sector.

The mission of Opportunity 2000 is to encourage companies and government agencies to set goals for increasing opportunities for women, particularly in management, by the year 2000. It assists the boards of directors of member organizations by offering practical techniques that can be used by their line managers. It provides publications, workshops, and research findings, and links organizations with human resource specialists. In essence, it is a national clearinghouse for firms that wish to utilize the abilities of their female personnel more fully. The United States has no such single clearinghouse.

Opportunity 2000 was created to carry out the EU directives. Membership is voluntary, but each member is required to pay a fee that covers the kinds of services mentioned above. In addition, member organizations are required to make three commitments:

- Develop clearly articulated organizational goals spelling out what will be accomplished for women.

- Publish organizational goals where they can be seen by the public, i.e., in ads, annual reports, etc.
- Monitor progress toward achievement of the stated goals and report on it publicly on a regular basis.

What is impressive about the Opportunity 2000 program is that it is not merely a set of ideological policies. It requires the articulation of specific goals and the measurement of their achievement. It is important to note that the program's rationale emphasizes business advantages rather than social equity:

- Improvement in customer/market orientation
- Offering women an employer of choice
- Reduction in organizational costs
- Increase in productivity
- Increase in creativity and innovation
- Development of individual potential

Opportunity 2000 distributes a brochure to its members that states, "Underutilization of the skill and talent of half the population and approximately 45% of the workforce is socially and economically wasteful, and unprofitable in business terms. Increased opportunity for women is central to organizational and business effectiveness." The brochure makes the following specific suggestions for bringing about change:

- Include discussions of progress on equal opportunity in the annual report to shareholders and in staff reports.
- Make reference to equal opportunity in the organization's mission statement.
- Appoint an equal opportunity champion at the board level to support equal opportunity practitioners.
- Ensure that external messages communicated through advertising, promotional materials, annual reports, etc., reflect internal goals.
- Require the monitoring of performance against equal

opportunity goals, and reward success appropriately and publicly.
• Set up a forum for dialogue between management and women in the organization.

Admittedly, Opportunity 2000 is only a few years old, and its success has yet to be proven in quantifiable terms. However, it has made at least some executives agree with Paul Southworth, president of Avon Cosmetics U.K., who says, "We need women to get competitive advantage."[14] In 1992 there were 140 member organizations in Opportunity 2000, employing more than 25 percent of the total U.K. workforce. Most member organizations have published goals and issued progress reports, and there are several success stories.

Barclays Bank PLC now offers a formal job-sharing program and private medical care for its part-time managers, many of whom are women. The bank has instituted a "responsibility break" that entitles those responsible for sick, elderly, or disabled relatives to take a complete leave or work part-time for up to six months. The bank's annual report contains a yearly progress report on women in the firm, something rarely found in U.S. annual reports. At the end of its first year in Opportunity 2000, Boots the Chemist, a major drugstore chain, had achieved its stated goal of increasing the number of women in supervisory, management, and senior positions. Shell U.K., a large oil company, has substantially reduced its female turnover rate. It has increased the number of women recruited, specified percentage targets for women, and developed action plans that are publicized internally and externally.

Although most Opportunity 2000 members are private sector corporations, government agencies also belong. One that provides a good case study of a major effort to address female underutilization is the National Health Service (NHS). This effort is particularly interesting since the NHS employs a very large number of professional women.

The NHS is the largest Opportunity 2000 member, and was the first to join the program. It is also the third-largest employer in the world, and the largest employer of women in Europe.[15] It has 1,000,000 employees, the vast majority of whom (750,000) are women. Eighty-three percent of the top management posts are held by men. Not only is there a considerable difference in the way men and women are represented in NHS management, but access to senior management has historically been discriminatory.[16] In the area of nursing, 90 percent of the qualified nurses are women, but 45 percent of the chief nursing officers are men.[17] Although 61 percent of the NHS finance staff are women, they hold only 9 percent of top-grade finance director posts in health authorities and trusts.[18]

In 1982 Prime Minister Margaret Thatcher said, "The battle for women's rights has been largely won."[19] A decade later Martin Whitfield, labor correspondent for the *Independent*, said, "The Civil Service has failed in its objective set eight years ago to promote women to the highest jobs."[20] Regardless of whose comment best describes women in the United Kingdom, there is widespread agreement that new winds have been blowing since April 1991, when Prime Minister John Major's secretary of state for health, Virginia Bottomley, created a Women's Unit in the NHS.

The Women's Unit is primarily responsible for the Opportunity 2000 effort in the NHS, and operates in conjunction with the U.K. Equal Opportunities Commission. A prime objective of its program is to utilize female physicians more fully and to increase the number of women general managers from 18 percent to 30 percent.[21] The program is well on its way to seeing its goals realized. Caroline Langridge, director of the NHS Women's Unit, is dedicated to making sure the objective is reached, and her commitment has much to do with the program's success so far. There is a strong emphasis on management training. Valerie Hammond, chief executive of the Roffey Park Management Institute, Dr. Beverly Alimo-Metcalfe of the Nuffield Institute for Health at the University of Leeds, and Ann James, formerly of the Kings Fund College, have been key players in the research and training effort at the NHS.

The NHS program has a number of initiatives, one of which is a National Career Development Register that identifies senior women managers who wish to compete for top management posts. Women on the register are helped by career development managers to ensure their advancement to key positions in the NHS. In its first year, of about five hundred women on the register, eighty-four were promoted, forty-nine of them (10 percent) to board-level posts.[22] This innovative program is a model of proactive career development for women.

All NHS employees receive a guide to Opportunity 2000, which spells out in detail the goals of the program. It is an attempt to introduce all one million employees to the agency's emphasis on equal opportunity efforts. It includes a section titled "What about Men?" that explains how men too can take advantage of the chance to balance work and family better by supporting Opportunity 2000 goals.

A possible indication of the success of Opportunity 2000 at the NHS is that there appears to be a growing resistance to the program on the part of top male executives. Such resistance, or male backlash, is generally not seen until major changes are taking place and the status quo is challenged. Ann James, who helped train potential women leaders at the NHS, says, "This effort is much harder than we thought. We didn't expect the backlash."[23] Caroline Langridge did, however. "The implementation of Opportunity 2000 coincided with the U.K. recession and a real contraction in top management posts at the NHS, leading to the inevitable backlash," she says. "More surprisingly, men, impressed by the results, have now demanded access to the same action programmes run for women. In this case, imitation is the sincerest form of flattery."[24]

While it is too soon to know whether the NHS Opportunity 2000 program will translate into economic competition for the United States, the effort is worth watching. If the largest government bureaucracy in the United Kingdom can effectively tap into its women employees by creating an environment where women are valued, that may prove to be an important lesson for American organizations.

Japan

In Japan, there is no Glass Ceiling Commission, no Opportunity 2000, no other similar effort to address the underutilization of professional women. An Equal Employment Opportunity Law was passed in 1986 and is often cited by Japanese executives as an indication of their interest in this issue. However, since there are no sanctions for noncompliance, its value is somewhat questionable. Similarly, although 90 percent of all Japanese companies offer childcare leave, almost 60 percent of these companies report that they haven't had a single request for leave since the universal childcare leave law was enacted in April 1992.[25]

The issue of employee rights is new in Japan, but there is an increasing awareness that international standards regarding the treatment of women will force Japan to change. The labor shortage and a shift in employee attitudes are also contributing to a transformation of Japan's work environment. The concept of lifetime employment is collapsing, and seniority-based practices are disappearing. All these changes will require a new focus on human resource policy, which will have a profound impact on future employment practices in Japan.[26]

Japanese executives are noticing an increase in requests from career women in their companies to be assigned abroad. Michiyo Kozaki, a twenty-eight-year-old sales executive at the Hong Kong branch of a Japanese furniture concern, is a case in point. To get the job she wanted, she left Japan. Many Japanese professional women are going to Hong Kong, where they feel that they are respected because their talents are needed. "Between 1991 and 1993, the number of Japanese women in Hong Kong jumped by nearly 25% to 7,381, according to the most recent data available from the Japanese consulate in Hong Kong," reports the *Wall Street Journal*.[27] At the same time, more and more American women are pursuing positions outside the United States because they feel international experience is necessary for top-level positions.[28] Professional women in all countries are becoming more internationally mobile. They are shopping around the world for positions that best take advantage of their abilities and prepare them for a job market where international experience is increasingly important.

The number of Japanese women with career aspirations is relatively small. This is not surprising, since Japan is a country where being dutiful wives and daughters is still considered the proper role of women. However, this too is changing. Women have always worked in Japan, but not in professional or managerial positions. What is changing is the type of women who work and the reasons they work. Historically, women worked on farms and in small shops, places where they could keep an eye on their children, which was their primary task. Fully employed women with high school or college diplomas, called "salary girls" or "business girls," have mostly been young and single. Women traditionally quit their jobs as soon as they got married, for once a woman married (and most did until recently), her career was considered over.[29] Today, however, the number of women entering medicine, law, the civil service, business, and engineering is increasing, and women are working not only for economic survival but because they desire a career. There is evidence that large Japanese firms are beginning to offer women career opportunities.[30] This development may be related to a long-term labor shortage; some observers believe that Japanese executives would rather promote Japanese women than hire male foreigners.

Still, Lewis Steel, an attorney who represents plaintiffs in sex discrimination cases brought against Japanese firms, says that Japanese executives "treat women like office flowers."[31] Men are clearly directed into generalist career paths, and women into noncareer clerical paths.[32] Japanese women professionals say men are given better assignments and rotations, and have more opportunities to establish important business relationships through socializing after work. Like their American counterparts, but to an even greater degree, they feel that the abilities of women are usually overlooked or discounted.

Japanese women who are married and have children are the most likely to feel underutilized, while those who are single are the least likely. This makes sense, since married women are assumed to be "drop-outs" in the Japanese management culture, where marriage is a much greater deterrent to career success than in the United States and the EU countries. However, this is slowly changing, and even Japanese men are beginning to disregard traditional work/family customs. Also, Japanese women are delaying marriage, and a new term, *kekkon shinai kamoshiranai shokogun* ("I might not get married"), has emerged.[33] The implication is that Japanese women may be sacrificing family for career, as American women began to do in the 1970s. In any case, a few large firms have begun to recognize the need to attract and retain female employees and have built on-site day care centers.[34]

The fact that the Japanese princess, Masako Owada, was Harvard-trained, and was a highly successful career woman before marrying the Japanese prince, cannot be overlooked in the context of the changing view of professional women in Japan. All eyes are now on her to see how or if she will have an impact on the role of women in Japan. She donned the traditional gown for her marriage, but she talked longer than she was supposed to talk, and she is said to have extracted some promises about relaxing the constraints usually imposed on women in her position. Her popularity may be a sign of a major cultural change.[35]

Finally, one phenomenon that is often overlooked in discussions of Japan is the large number of women—

approximately 2,500,000—who own and run nonagricultural small businesses. Most of these businesses employ fewer than five workers, and many are family-owned shops. Nonetheless, the experience women gain in this type of endeavor provides them with a work ethic that is transferable.

Should the women of Japan begin to organize, their large numbers could have an impact on the innovativeness and productivity of Japanese business. The United States can't afford to ignore this possibility. The conversion of the talents of women into leadership skills may be Japan's competitive secret!

Comparative Perceptions of Female Underutilization

It is one thing to talk about concrete directives, goals, and programs. It is another to talk about perceptions, which are much more subjective. As I said in Chapter 4, the perceptions of men and women are often so different that it is as though they live in different cultures. Similarly, the perceptions of women in different countries differ because of cultural variations. Because "perception is reality" and as such motivates behavior, I surveyed women in the United States, Japan, Britain, and a few EU countries to find out how they perceived the underutilization issue.[36] Their responses support a few general observations.

American and British women said that "underutilization" means that one's skills and abilities are not being used. They made such comments as "Being given things to do that others with less education and ability could do," "Not being made responsible for tasks that capitalize on the best use of my skills and knowledge," and "Company sticks with job description/expectations rather than taking advantage of an individual's specific and unique talents and experience." EU women were briefer, mentioning "waste of resources" or "not taking advantage of abilities," usually without a gender connotation.

Japanese women tended to be very gender-specific. The word "woman" was in all of their responses, perhaps because they interpreted the question differently or because the unfamiliar word "underutilization" was somehow assumed to be connected to the plight of women. "Fewer opportunities are given women than men" was a common response. One female Japanese executive said, "The company doesn't expect knowledge, skills, or abilities from women." Another said, "The same type of job is not assigned to a woman in comparison with a man of the same age, education, and ability." A number of Japanese women who had been asked to perform "beverage service" (making and serving tea to men) gave this as an illustration of underutilization, something that requires little talent and is not expected of men.

When asked whether they felt personally underutilized, most American and European women said yes. German women were most likely to say no or to make light of the problem. As one German woman said, "Whenever I felt underutilized, I switched jobs." In other words, if a woman is underutilized, all she has to do is leave.

The few Japanese women who said they didn't feel underutilized may have been operating on the "relative deprivation" theory.[37] That is, compared to most women in Japan, women with some kind of career probably feel they are in a good place. Since most Japanese working women still find themselves performing "beverage service," those who don't may think their true talents have been recognized. On the other hand, they still feel devalued. "While I have to do clerical work and chores like serving tea to guests, photocopying, and filing," one respondent said, "men with much less experience don't have to." Most of the Japanese women said the workplace remains *otoko no shakai*, a man's world.

There were many responses to the survey question

about how underutilization should be measured. While there was no widely agreed-upon method of measurement, there was a sense that performance appraisals are currently made by those least able to determine individual potential, namely, bosses. Why? Because they only take a narrow look at what is being done. The people whose abilities are being assessed are the people most likely to know what talents they have and how those talents could be effectively used, yet they are the least likely to be consulted. EU women's responses were less detailed than those from other countries, consistent with their other responses about the underutilization issue. But EU women did suggest that employees be asked whether they feel all their skills are being used.

The Japanese responses to the measurement question were extremely vague. A number of respondents said utilization should be measured by "counting the numbers of women." Since the Japanese culture tends to view performance in group rather than individual terms, Japanese women may not think about measuring individual potential. However, knowing how many women there are in some given position or organization does not tell us much about whether or how their talents are being used.

The question about what needs to be done to address female underutilization elicited many answers from American and British women. They mentioned the need to increase family support systems such as childcare, flextime, and job sharing, but they also called for major organizational changes, including performance standards that recognize female as well as male work characteristics, ways of organizing work so that part-time employment is not seen as second-rate, equal educational and training opportunities, and changes in hierarchical structures that limit women's career development.

The responses of EU women were more general and more related to major cultural change. For example, one woman simply said, "Education," another said, "Stop worrying about women's development, start worrying about attitudes of young men," and a third said, "Place women in more decision centers." Such comments suggest that EU women are not yet thinking much about the economic underutilization of women.

Japanese women had many insightful suggestions for change, ranging from "termination of traditional sex roles and the seniority system" to a demand that men "change their values and increase their understanding of working women" to a request for "changes in ways jobs are assigned and performance is appraised." Other responses, such as "Professional jobs should be available on a part-time basis" and "Both men and women have to work less and balance work and family," are consistent with recent newspaper stories indicating that not all women in Japan are willing to play traditional female roles. "Rushing into marriage is especially hazardous these days because men's and women's expectations are diverging," reports a *Wall Street Journal* article. "The typical young man here still wants a girl like mom, who will raise his kids and tend to his needs, but many women are seeking a new deal."[38]

The results of my informal survey reinforce the main message of this book: that women, men, and organizations have to change if the talents of women are to be utilized more fully and the United States is to secure a competitive lead. Although America appears to have a head start in the race to leverage the abilities of women, there is no guarantee that it will win the race. The EU's increasingly strong effort to ensure equal opportunities for women is being translated into private initiatives that may ultimately change the way women are valued in those countries. The implications of such a change cannot be overlooked.

The United States, meanwhile, is resting on its laurels. Much like IBM in the 1970s, it seems sure of its lead. U.S. organizations are not looking hard enough over their shoulder to see who's behind, or far enough into the future to see what lies ahead. The United States is watching Japan, but not primarily in a human resource utilization context.

It sees a government and corporate establishment with no major plans to enlist women in the labor force. It knows that Japanese corporations rarely enforce equal opportunity programs for women. And while Japanese officials proudly point to their equal opportunity law, it is no secret that there are no sanctions for noncompliance.

The women's movement, the accessibility of public and private education, and strong affirmative action efforts since the 1970s are among the factors that have created a climate more hospitable to professional women in the United States than in Western Europe and Japan. However, as I have said, new winds are blowing around the world. If the United States doesn't hoist a weather vane, those winds could scatter its advantage in the global competition for human resources.

What It All Means

American women possess leadership abilities that are particularly effective in today's organizations, yet their abilities remain undervalued and underutilized. In the future, what will distinguish one organization and one country from another will be its use of human resources. Today human resource utilization is not only a matter of social justice but a bottom-line issue.

A colleague of mine, Professor Alladi Venkatesh, asked me why I chose "competitive" rather than "collaborative" to describe America's secret. He suggested that "competitive" implies maleness and reinforces the one-best-model mindset. In a sense he is correct. Competition is associated with the one best model, and modern economic systems are based on competitiveness and social Darwinism. However, it's altogether possible that competition and collaboration are not as contradictory as was once thought. In the words of Susan Davis, the financial adviser whose company was described in Chapter 7, "Collaboration is the ultimate form of competition." Competition and collaboration need not be mutually exclusive. The fact that General Electric tries to sell more dishwashers than KitchenAid is not a gender issue; it has to do with profits. General Electric and Kitchen-Aid compete for sales, but they share trade association resources such as demographic data and political lobbyists. Similarly, in the realm of international relations, where competitiveness is key, there is a history of cooperation and collaboration in such areas as agriculture, health, and pollution control. Today alliances, networks, and partnerships are seen as fundamental rather than tangential to economic success.

The interaction between men and women in organizations can be likened to the interaction between companies and countries that compete and cooperate at the same time. The international automobile industry is a case in point. American cars were once made entirely in the United States. Japanese cars were made in Japan. Now it is difficult to tell where the parts in American and Japanese cars were manufactured or assembled. Car making has become an international collaborative process packaged in a national competitive wrapper. Similarly, men and women working together in managerial positions can constitute an impressive competitive force.

I must repeat that gender issues are a subset of cultural diversity issues. I am emphatically not urging the fuller utilization of women at the expense of other historically devalued groups, or, for that matter, of qualified white males. Nor am I proposing a new best model based on female attributes that appear to be particularly effective in today's fast-changing global environment. The talents of women should be valued and used because they represent an economic resource. This is not to say that the talents of other groups are irrelevant or that the talents of men are obsolete. They, too, represent an economic resource.

Nowhere do I suggest that Alexis de Tocqueville was correct when he said, "If I were asked . . . to what the singular prosperity and growing strength of that people [the Americans] ought mainly to be attributed, I should reply:

To the superiority of their women."[1] I have tried to show that women are different from men, but not superior or inferior, and that the differences women bring to the workplace constitute an economic resource—an added value. In the previous chapters I have supplied evidence to suggest that women create work environments in which people can be themselves and don't have to "fit in" to a one best model of managerial behavior. I have said that women tend to feel comfortable with ambiguity, to be inclusive rather than exclusive, and to evaluate performance in both qualitative and quantitative terms. I have noted that women push for benefit programs responsive to a wide range of employee needs, and share power and information in a way that is conducive to shared responsibility. I have argued that because of these attributes, the admission of women to what historically has been an all-male domain—top management—results in higher morale, increased productivity, and greater innovation.

When I began this book three years ago, there was little discussion of human resources as a key factor in the development of management strategy. Human resource utilization was the concern of human resource departments, not CEOs. But as Philip Harris writes, "The leadership challenge in organizations today is to learn how to capitalize on human assets to enhance a system's effectiveness."[2] America's professional women are the biggest untapped vein of human assets in the world. As organizations struggle to adapt to a rapidly changing global environment, they would be well advised to recognize the link between management strategy, human resources, and the underutilization of women. When they do, they will have discovered America's competitive secret.

Too little attention has been paid to men's feelings and their relation to the discovery of this secret. The challenge to male self-esteem and the sense that men are losing power and control as they compete with women for leadership positions cannot be lightly dismissed. However, today male executives have an opportunity to profit from perceiving women as an economic resource rather than a problem. The question is, will they seize it? Will they come to agree with Edward Steichen, the famous photographer, that women are "the greatest undeveloped natural resource in the world today"?[3]

Notes

Chapter 1: The Bottom Line

1. Harlan Cleveland, "The Decision Makers," in *The Future Executive* (New York: Harper and Row, 1972), reprinted in *Center Magazine*, September–October 1973, 11.

2. Herbert A. Simon, "Making Management Decisions: The Role of Intuition and Emotion," *Academy of Management Executive*, February 1987, 57–63.

3. Peter Senge, *The Fifth Discipline* (New York: Doubleday, 1990).

4. See, for example, John Gardner, *Self Renewal* (New York: Harper and Row, 1963).

5. T. George Harris, "The Post-Capitalist Executive: An Interview with Peter F. Drucker," *Harvard Business Review*, May–June 1993, 115.

6. On the phenomenon of externalization, see Jeffrey Pfeffer, "Competitive Advantage through People," *California Management Review*, Winter 1994, 10.

7. Rosabeth Moss Kanter, "Collaborative Advantage: The Art of Alliances," *Harvard Business Review*, July–August 1994, 96–108.

8. Carol Hymowitz and Timothy D. Schellhardt, "The Glass Ceiling," in "The Corporate Woman: A Special Report," *Wall Street Journal*, March 24, 1986; "Glass Ceiling? It's More Like a Steel Cage," *Los Angeles Times*, March 20, 1995, B8.

9. "Workforce 2000: Work and Workers for the 21st Century, Executive Summary," Hudson Institute, June 1987.

10. "Human Capital," *Business Week*, September 19, 1988.

11. Michael E. Porter, *Competitive Strategy* (New York: Free Press, 1980).

12. See, for example, David Teece, Gary Pisano, and Amy Shuen, "Dynamic Capabilities and Strategic Management," working paper, University of California at Berkeley, 1992; Robert M. Grant, "The Resource Based Theory of Competitive Advantage: Implications for Strategy Formulation," 33 *California Management Review* (Spring 1991): 114–35; J. B. Barney, "Organizational Culture: Can It Be a Source of Sustained

Competitive Advantage?," *Academy of Management Review* 11 (1986): 656–65; and J. B. Barney, "Strategic Factors, Markets, Expectations, Luck, and Business Strategy," *Management Science* 42 (1986): 1211–41.

13. John A. Byrne, "Management's New Gurus," *Business Week*, August 31, 1992, 44–52.

14. Jeffrey Pfeffer, *Competitive Advantage through People* (Cambridge: Harvard Business School Press, 1994); Robert B. Reich, *The Work of Nations* (New York: Alfred A. Knopf, 1991).

15. Nancy K. Austin, "Motivating Employees without Pay or Promotions," *Working Woman*, November 1994, 18.

16. See, for example, Carol Gilligan, *In a Different Voice* (Cambridge: Harvard University Press, 1982); Mary Field Belenky et al., *Women's Ways of Knowing* (New York: Basic Books, 1986); Deborah Tannen, *You Just Don't Understand* (New York: William Morrow, 1990); John Gray, *Men Are from Mars, Women Are from Venus* (New York: HarperCollins, 1992).

17. James MacGregor Burns, *Leadership* (New York: Harper Torchbooks, 1978).

18. See Bernard Bass, *Handbook of Leadership* (New York: Free Press, 1974), 59–88.

19. Judy B. Rosener, "Ways Women Lead," *Harvard Business Review*, November–December 1990, 119–25.

20. Mary Midyette asked me not to identify the company but gave me permission to quote from her resignation letter.

21. This ad appeared in many general publications in late 1994.

22. J. Michael Cook, "Women in the Work Force—A Business Imperative," speech delivered at Los Angeles Town Hall, October 4, 1994.

23. Hardwick Simmons, conversation with author, October 31, 1994.

24. Quoted in Margaret Wente, "Women in Power, and the Paths They Took," *National Centre for Management Research and Development Newsletter*, August–September 1994.

25. Rafik Loutfy, conversation with author, October 31, 1994.

26. *BIM Sounding Board*, a Shell U.K. newsletter, date unknown.

Chapter 2: The One Best Model

1. Bernard M. Bass, *Bass & Stogdill's Handbook of Leadership*, 3d ed. (New York: Free Press, 1990).

2. Ibid., xii.

3. W. M. Ouchi, *Theory Z: How American Business Can Meet the Japanese Challenge* (Reading, Mass.: Addison-Wesley, 1981).

4. This conversation took place in July 1993. The man asked me not to use his name or the name of his firm.

5. Korn/Ferry International with the UCLA Anderson Graduate School of Management, *The Executive Profile: A Decade of Change in Corporate Leadership*, 1990.

6. Marilyn Loden and Judy Rosener, *Workforce America! Managing Employee Diversity as a Vital Resource* (Homewood, Ill.: Business One Irwin, 1991), 42–44.

7. Julie Newcomb Hill, conversation with author, August 1994.

8. See, for example, Margaret Hennig and Ann Jardim, *The Managerial Woman* (New York: Pocket Books, 1976); Betty Lehan Harragan, *Games Mother Never Taught You* (New York: Warner Books, 1977); Bette Ann Stead, *Women in Management* (Englewood Cliffs: Prentice Hall, 1978); Alice G. Sargent, *Beyond Sex Roles* (St. Paul: West Publishing, 1977, 1985); Ann Harriman, *Women/Men/Management* (New York: Praeger, 1985); Lynda L. Moore, *Not As Far As You Think* (Lexington, Mass.: Lexington Books/D. C. Heath, 1986).

9. Henry Mintzberg, *The Nature of Managerial Work* (New York: Harper and Row, 1973), vii–x.

10. Sally Helgeson, *The Female Advantage: Women's Ways of Leadership* (New York: Doubleday/Currency, 1990), 10, 20.

11. Arlie Hochschild with Anne Machung, *The Second Shift: Working Women and the Revolution at Home* (New York: Viking, 1989).

12. See Carol Gilligan, *In a Different Voice* (Cambridge: Harvard University Press, 1982); Mary Field Belenky et al., *Women's Ways of Knowing* (New York: Basic Books, 1986).

13. Rafik Loutfy, conversation with author, October 31, 1994.

14. I conducted this survey as part of a larger comparative survey done in cooperation with European Women's Management Development. See below, Chapter 10, n. 36.

15. Sarah Warmington, conversation with author, Los Angeles, July 1993.

16. "Change Sex through Surgery," *Los Angeles Times*, July 25, 1988, 14.

17. Sharon Timmer, conversation with author, Camden, Maine, September 1992.

18. Rosabeth Moss Kanter, *Men and Women of the Corporation* (New York: Basic Books, 1977), 206–42.

19. See, for example, "Women in the Profession—1994," *CPA Personnel Report* 12, no. 6 (June 1994): 5.

20. Valerie O'Donnell, conversation with author, Chicago, 1993.

21. Joline Godfrey, conversation with author, June 28, 1994. See also Godfrey's study of female entrepreneurs, *Our Wildest Dreams* (New York: HarperCollins, 1992).

22. Susanne Wedemeyer, "Result of PTEWAA [Pacific Telesis Em-

ployees for Women's Affirmative Action] Survey," *PTEWAA Newsletter*, July–August 1992, 2–3.

23. I spoke with this former student, who asked to remain anonymous, in July 1993.

24. This lawyer asked that her name not be used but offered this comment in a letter to me dated August 23, 1994.

25. "Daughter Battling Parents over Firm Sees 'Sexist Bias,'" *Wall Street Journal*, May 27, 1992.

Chapter 3: The Underutilization of Women

1. I sent questionnaires to approximately two hundred middle and upper managers during the months of January–June 1993, using a list of my personal contacts.

2. National Science Foundation, *Characteristics of Doctoral Scientists and Engineers in the United States, 1989* (Washington, D.C.: Government Printing Office, 1991), NSF91-317.

3. *Statistical Abstract of the United States, 1993*, 415, 405–7.

4. National Science Board, *Science and Engineering Indicators, 1989*, 72.

5. *Statistical Abstract, 1993*, 402.

6. See Polly Callahan and Heidi Hartmann, *Contingent Work* (Washington, D.C.: Economic Policy Institute, 1991).

7. Statistics for 1991 from National Center for Education Statistics, U.S. Department of Education, *Digest of Education Statistics, 1994*, NCES 94-115, 273; statistics for 1993 from Bureau of Labor Statistics, U.S. Department of Labor, *Employment and Earnings*, January 1994, 243.

8. *Cracking the Glass Ceiling: Strategies for Success* (New York: Catalyst, 1994); Korn/Ferry International with the UCLA Anderson Graduate School of Management, *Decade of the Executive Woman, 1993*; U.S. Department of Labor, "A Report on the Glass Ceiling Initiative" (Washington, D.C.: Government Printing Office, 1991).

9. See Margaret Karsten, *Management and Gender* (Westport, Conn.: Quorum Books, 1994), 13; and Patricia Aburdene and John Naisbitt, *Megatrends for Women* (New York: Villard Books, 1992), 61.

10. Aburdene and Naisbitt, *Megatrends*, 79.

11. "Women in the Profession—1994," *CPA Personnel Report* 12, no. 6 (June 1994).

12. Lori Bongiorno, "Where Are All the Female B-School Profs?" *Business Week*, November 7, 1992.

13. Jane Gross, "Female Surgeon's Quitting Touches Nerve at Medical Schools," *New York Times*, July 13, 1991, B1.

14. Judy B. Rosener, "Ways Women Lead," *Harvard Business Review*, November–December 1990, 119–25; Dawn-Mare Driscoll and Carol R. Goldberg, *Members of the Club* (New York: Free Press, 1993).

15. "Women on the Board," USA Snapshots, *USA Today*, March 15, 1994.

16. Meredith K. Wadman, "Often Belittled by Their Male Colleagues, Women Doctors Also Find Pay Disparity," *Wall Street Journal*, November 25, 1992.

17. Laura Mansnerus, "Why Women Are Leaving the Law," *Working Woman*, April 1993.

18. "A Question of Equity," report to the President and the Congress of the United States by the U.S. Merit Systems Protection Board, October 1992, ix.

19. Boyce Rensberger, "Breaking Down Science's Old Boy Network," *Washington Post National Weekly*, August 31–September 6, 1992, 33.

20. Myra H. Strober, "Gender and Occupational Segregation," *International Encyclopedia of Education*, 2d ed. (Oxford, England: Pergamon Press, 1994), 2427–28.

21. Ibid.

22. Gross, "Female Surgeon's Quitting Touches Nerve."

23. Clifford Adelman, *Paradoxes of Attainment*, U.S. Department of Education, June 1991.

24. "Facts on Work of Women," *Statistical Abstract of the United States, 1991*, 417.

25. Wadman, "Women Doctors Also Find Pay Disparity."

26. *Working Woman*, 1993 Salary Survey, January 1993.

27. Ibid., 28.

28. Faye J. Crosby, *Relative Deprivation and Working Women* (New York: Oxford University Press, 1982).

29. Diane Harris et al., "Does Your Pay Measure Up?" *Working Woman*, January 1994, 26–27.

30. For a summary of comparable worth, see Francine D. Blau and Marianne A. Ferber, *The Economics of Women, Men, and Work* (Englewood Cliffs: Prentice Hall, 1992), 227.

31. Harris et al., "Does Your Pay Measure Up?" 26–27.

32. Rosener, "Ways Women Lead," 120, 121.

33. For a discussion of career investment theories, see Blau and Ferber, *Economics of Women and Men*, 146–48.

34. Ibid., 217. See also Myra Strober, "The MBA Degree: Same Passport to Success for Women and Men?" in Phyllis Wallace, ed., *Women in the Workplace* (Boston: Auburn House, 1982); and Harris et al., "Does Your Pay Measure Up?"

35. See "Why Women and Minorities Make Less Progress in Their

Careers Than White Males," memorandum, Organization Resources Counselors, New York, August 26, 1992.

36. For more on this point, see Rita Mae Kelly, *The Gendered Economy* (Newbury Park, Calif.: Sage, 1991), 141–52.

37. Helen Astin, "The Meaning of Work in Women's Lives: A Socio-psychological Model of Career Choice and Work Behavior," *Counseling Psychologist* 12: 117–26.

38. Victor Fuchs, *Women's Quest for Economic Equality* (Cambridge: Harvard University Press, 1988).

39. Veronica F. Nieva and Barbara A. Gutek, *Women and Work: A Psychological Perspective* (New York: Praeger, 1992). See also Gregory B. Northcraft and Barbara A. Gutek, "Point-Counterpoint: Discrimination against Women in Management—Going, Going, Gone or Going but Never Gone?" in Ellen A. Fagenson, ed., *Women in Management* (Newbury Park, Calif.: Sage, 1993), 219–45.

40. Arlie Hochschild with Anne Machung, *The Second Shift: Working Women and the Revolution at Home* (New York: Viking, 1989).

41. Lotte Bailyn, *Breaking the Mold* (New York: Free Press, 1993), 122.

42. Felice Schwartz, "Management Women and the New Facts of Life," *Harvard Business Review*, January–February 1989.

43. For a discussion of this view, see Blau and Ferber, *Economics of Women and Men*, 149–51.

44. See, for example, Cynthia Cockburn, *In the Way of Women* (Ithaca: ILR Press, 1991), 9.

45. This point is made very effectively in Anne Fausto-Sterling, *Myths of Gender* (New York: Basic Books, 1985), 22.

46. Carol Tavris, *The Mismeasure of Woman* (New York: Simon & Schuster, 1992), 15–25.

Chapter 4: Sexual Static

1. Judy B. Rosener, "Coping With Sexual Static," Business World, *New York Times Magazine*, December 7, 1986.

2. Carol Hymowitz and Timothy D. Schellhardt, "The Glass Ceiling," *Wall Street Journal*, March 24, 1986.

3. For just a few examples, excluding numberless articles in newspapers and magazines, see Barbara A. Gutek, *Sex in the Workplace* (San Francisco: Jossey-Bass, 1985); Lisa A. Maniero, *Office Romance: Love, Power, and Sex in the Workplace* (Rawson Associates, 1989); Patrice D. and Jack C. Horn, *Sex in the Office* (Reading, Mass.: Addison-Wesley, 1982); and Robert E. Quinn, "Coping with Cupid: The Formation, Impact, and Management of Romantic Relationships in Organizations," *Administrative Science Quarterly* 22 (March 1977): 30–45.

4. Jean Lipman-Blumen, *Gender Roles and Power* (Englewood Cliffs: Prentice Hall, 1984), 54.

5. Ibid., 59.

6. Susan Harter and Christine Chao, "The Role of Competence in Children's Creation of Imaginary Friends," *Merrill-Palmer Quarterly* 38, no. 3 (June 1992): 350–63.

7. Gutek, *Sex in the Workplace*, 15–16.

8. See R. A. Wicklund and J. W. Brehm, *Perspectives on Cognitive Dissonance* (Hillsdale, N.J.: Erlbaum, 1976).

9. Deborah Tannen, *You Just Don't Understand* (New York: William Morrow, 1990).

10. John Gray, *Men Are from Mars, Women Are from Venus* (New York: HarperCollins, 1992).

11. See, for example, Jo Durden Smith and Diane Desimone, *Sex and the Brain* (New York: Arbor House, 1983); Anne Moir and David Jessel, *Brain Sex* (New York: Carol Publishing Group, 1991); Edith Weiner and Arnold Brown, *Office Biology* (New York: Master Media, 1993).

12. Dr. Joe E. Bogen, conversation with author, January 30, 1993.

13. Jerre Levy, "Lateral Specialization of the Human Brain: Behavioral Manifestations and Possible Evolutionary Basis," in J. A. Kiger, ed., *The Biology of Behavior* (Eugene: University of Oregon Press, 1972); Doreen Kimura, "Are Men's and Women's Brains Really Different?" *Canadian Psychology* 28, no. 2 (1987): 133.

14. Smith and Desimone, *Sex and the Brain*, 76; Anne Fausto-Sterling, *Myths of Gender* (New York: Basic Books, 1985), 38; "Sizing the Sexes," *Time*, January 20, 1992, 42.

15. Doreen Kimura, "How Different Are Male and Female Brains?" *Orbit* (Ontario Institute for Studies in Education) 17, no. 3 (October 1986): 13–14.

16. Lipman-Blumen, *Gender Roles and Power*, 91–96.

17. Clifford R. Geertz, *The Interpretation of Cultures* (New York: Basic Books, 1973).

18. "Subculture implies that the group shares some of the larger national culture, but has some values or customs that differ from the larger culture." William B. Gudykunst, *Bridging Differences* (Newbury Park, Calif.: Sage, 1991), 44.

Chapter 5: How Men Feel

1. Greg Howard and Craig MacIntosh, *Sally Forth*, in the *Los Angeles Times*, April 7, 1994.

2. On the relation of work and self-image for men, see Michael S. Kimmel, ed., *Changing Men: New Directions in Research on Men and Masculinity* (Newbury Park, Calif.: Sage, 1987).

3. Talcott Parsons, "Age and Sex in the Social Structure of the United States," in Clyde Kluckhohn and Henry A. Murray, eds., *Personality in Nature, Society, and Culture* (New York: Alfred A. Knopf, 1949), 273.

4. Michael S. Kimmel, "What Do Men Want?" *Harvard Business Review*, November–December 1983, 50–63.

5. The study was conducted between January 1993 and February 1994. Calls were made to approximately two hundred men in a wide variety of professions and industries in ten states. The men were informed that the conversations were not being taped but that I would be taking notes, and that their names would not be used.

6. Marilyn and David Machlowitz, "Hug by the Boss Could Lead to a Slap from the Judge," *Wall Street Journal*, August 25, 1986.

7. Sherwood Ross, "Few Men Take Advantage of Family-Leave Policies," *Orange County Register*, January 15, 1993.

8. Colin Harrison, "Here's Baby. Dad Stays Home. Dad Gets Antsy," *New York Times*, August 31, 1993.

9. Sue Saellenbarger, "Men Become Evasive about Family Demands," Work and Family, *Wall Street Journal*, August 16, 1991.

10. Audrey Freedman, "Those Costly Good Old Boys," *New York Times*, July 12, 1989.

11. Judy B. Rosener and Lyman Porter, pilot study on sexual static in single-sex and mixed-sex audit teams, University of California, Irvine, 1987.

12. Quoted in Michele Galen and Ann Therese Palmer, "White, Male, and Worried," *Business Week*, January 31, 1994, 50–55.

13. Lyn Kathlene, "Power and Influence in State Legislative Policymaking: The Interaction of Gender and Position in Committee Hearing Debates," *American Political Science Review* 88, no. 3 (September 1994): 1–17.

14. Peggy McIntosh, "White Privilege and Male Privilege: A Personal Account of Coming to See Correspondences through Work in Women's Studies," working paper 189, Wellesley College, Center for Research on Women, 1988.

15. Galen and Palmer, "White, Male, and Worried."

16. Rochelle Sharpe, "The Waiting Game," *Wall Street Journal*, March 29, 1994.

17. Joe Bob Briggs, *Iron Joe Bob* (New York: Atlantic Monthly Press, 1992).

18. Joan E. Rigdon, "A Wife's Higher Pay Can Test a Marriage," *Wall Street Journal*, January 28, 1993.

19. I am indebted to Joe Flowers, co-author of *Age Wave* and author of *Prince of the Magic Kingdom: Michael Eisner and the Re-making of Disney*, for his insights about men, which are reflected in this paragraph.

20. Harris Sussman, conversation with author, Dallas, January 12, 1993.

21. Joseph H. Pleck, "Men's Power with Women, Other Men, and Society," in Michael S. Kimmel and Michael A. Messner, eds., *Men's Lives*, 2d ed. (New York: Macmillan, 1992), 21.

22. Ibid., 22.

23. Mike McNeil, conversation with author, January 1994.

24. Alphonso Brown, conversation with author, February 1994.

25. Dorothy J. Gaiter, "Black Women's Gains in Corporate America Outstrip Black Men's," *Wall Street Journal*, March 8, 1994.

26. Anthony Astrachan, *How Men Feel* (New York: Anchor, 1988), 172–73.

27. Duncan H. Spelman, "White Men and Managing Diversity," *Diversity Factor*, Spring 1993, 13.

Chapter 6: How Women React

1. Quoted in Amanda Troy Segal and Wendy Zellner, "Corporate Women," *Business Week*, June 8, 1992, 74.

2. *EEOC v AT&T*, 365 F Supp 1105, 1121 (ED Pa 1973) (Higginbotham, J.) modified 506 F 2d 735 (3d cir 1974).

3. "Sex Discrimination? It Happens Only to Others, Many Women Say," *Wall Street Journal*, Labor Letter section, January 25, 1994.

4. Judy B. Rosener, "'Corporate Flight' and Female Entrepreneurs: Is There a Connection?," unpublished working paper, Graduate School of Management, University of California, Irvine, November 1989. The study consisted of a written questionnaire given to 125 attendees at a one-day conference for women entrepreneurs.

5. Judy B. Rosener, "The Retention of Women and People of Color: Are We Asking the Right Questions?," issue paper prepared for the 1990 All-University Faculty Conference on Graduate Student and Faculty Affirmative Action, University of California, Irvine; and Bernice R. Sandler Project on the Status and Education of Women, "The Campus Climate Revisited: Chilly for Women Faculty, Administrators, and Graduate Students," Association of American Colleges, October 1986.

6. Lee Butler, "The Anatomy of Collusive Behavior," *NTL Connections* 4, no. 1 (December 1987): 2.

7. Michelle Levander, "Dishing It Out and Taking It," *San Jose Mercury News*, June 10, 1991.

8. This account is based on information sent to me by Linda Cyrog-Giacomi, now vice president of business planning, American President Companies, Ltd.

9. John Lillie, fax to author, June 13, 1994.

10. Nancy Barry, conversation with author, New York, 1993.

11. Frances K. Conley, M.D., "Confessions of an Academic Maverick," *Commonwealth*, November 1991, 778–87; and conversation with author, August 1993.

12. Joline Godfrey, *Our Wildest Dreams* (New York: HarperCollins, 1992).

13. "Women-owned Businesses: The New Economic Force," National Foundation for Women Business Owners data report, 1992; NFWBO biennial membership survey, 1993; and "Women-owned Business: The New Economic Force," NFWBO fact sheet, 1993.

14. Tamar Lewin, "Accountant Wins Suit on Sex Bias," *New York Times*, December 6, 1990.

15. Natalie J. Sokoloff, *Black Women and White Women in the Professions* (New York: Routledge, 1992), 19.

16. Sokoloff, *Black Women and White Women*, 94; and Leon E. Wynter, "Double Whammy Hinders 'Double Minorities,'" *Wall Street Journal*, Business and Race section, January 19, 1994.

17. Ella Louise Bell, "Myths, Stereotypes, and Realities of Black Women: A Personal Reflection," *Journal of Applied Behavioral Science* 28, no. 3 (September 1992): 363–76; S. M. Nkomo, "The Emperor Has No Clothes: Rewriting 'Race in Organizations,'" *Academy of Management Journal* 17 (1992): 487–513. See also Cheryl Townsend Gilkes, "'Liberated to Work Like Dogs!' Labeling Black Women—Their Work," in H. Grossman and N. Chester, eds., *The Experience and Meaning of Work in Women's Lives* (Hillside, N.J.: Erlbaum, 1990), 165–87.

18. Sokoloff, *Black and White Women*, 94.

19. Segal and Zellner, "Corporate Women," 82.

20. Sokoloff, *Black and White Women*, 93.

21. Terri A. Scandura and Melenie J. Lankau, "The Effects of Flexible Work Hours on Organizational Commitment: A Matched Sample Investigation of Female and Male Executives," paper presented at National Academy of Management annual meeting, August 1993.

22. See, for example, Dalia Etzion and Ayala Pines, "Sex and Culture as Factors Explaining Reported Coping Behavior and Burnout Levels of Human Service Professionals: A Social Psychological Perspective," Israel Institute of Business Research, Tel Aviv University, working paper 696/81, November 1981.

Chapter 7: The Impact Women Make

1. I first interviewed Judith Rogala at the National Conference of the International Women's Forum in San Antonio, Texas, in the fall of 1993. I have had subsequent telephone conversations and correspondence with her.

2. Rosabeth Moss Kanter, "Some Effects of Proportion on Group Life: Skewed Sex Ratios and Responses to Token Women," *American Journal of Sociology* 82: 965–91.

3. "Women in Congress Hail Big Gains of '93," *Los Angeles Times*, December 3, 1993.

4. Carol Kleiman, "Women Executives Find Power in the Threes," *Chicago Tribune*, January 18, 1993.

5. Susan E. Tiffet, "Board Gains," *Working Woman*, February 1994, 70.

6. Shirley Cheramy, fax to author, March 22, 1995.

7. "Do Women Help Women? Don't Bet on Some at Top," *Wall Street Journal*, March 29, 1994.

8. Nancy Woodhull, conversations with author, July 1991, December 1993, and May 1994.

9. Quoted in Lucy Kellaway, "Female Progress by the Book," *Financial Times*, July 14, 1993.

10. Quoted in Doron P. Levin, "Honda Names Woman to Head Plant in Ohio," *New York Times*, November 24, 1992.

11. "How World's Top Woman Ad Executive Hit the Heights," *New York Times*, May 4, 1992.

12. See Rita Mae Kelly, *The Gendered Economy* (Newbury Park, Calif.: Sage, 1991), 100.

13. Beth Reingold, "Representing Women: Gender Differences among Arizona and California State Legislators" (Ph.D. dissertation, University of California, Berkeley, 1992).

14. Lyn Kathlene, "Studying the New Voice of Women in Politics," *Chronicle of Higher Education*, November 18, 1992.

15. Katherine S. Mangan, "First Female Law Dean in Texas Is a Change Agent," *Chronicle of Higher Education*, January 8, 1992.

16. Tiffet, "Board Changes," 38.

17. Kate Bednarski, "Convincing Male Managers to Target Women Customers," *Working Woman*, June 1993.

18. Andrea Heiman, "Beyond Thinking Pink," *Los Angeles Times*, June 2, 1992; Larry Armstrong, "Women Power at Mazda," *Business Week*, September 21, 1992, 84; Warren Brown, "In the Driver's Seat of Automotive Design," *Washington Post*, National Weekly Edition, January 3–9, 1994, 19.

19. Terry Savage, "Another First for the First Woman of Wall Street," *Chicago Sun Times*, December 20, 1992.

20. Matthew Schifrin, "Children's TV Gets Smart," *Lear's*, June 1993, 24–25.

21. Carol Gilligan, *In a Different Voice* (Cambridge: Harvard University Press, 1982), 7–8.

22. These observations were made by Lynn Rosener, an educational

software designer and usability specialist with the Learning Company in Fremont, California. She works with boys and girls to see how they react to various software programs. See also Susan Morse, "Why Girls Don't Like Computer Games," *AAUW Outlook*, Winter 1995, 16–19.

23. Conversation between author and corporate manager who asked not to be identified.

24. Susan Davis, conversation with author, Newport Beach, California, September 1994.

25. Quoted in On the Record section, *Redbook*, undated clipping.

26. Larry King, CNN newscast, January 9, 1994.

27. Lyn L. Kathlene, "Alternative Views of Crime: Legislative Policy-making in Gendered Terms," paper presented at the annual meeting of the Midwest Political Science Association, Chicago, Illinois, April 18–20, 1991.

28. "Gramm Calls Reno 'Sweet' but a Poor Fit," *Orange County Register*, January 22, 1994.

29. "How Men and Women Perceive and Act—The Theme of Bank's 'No Holds Barred' Session," *Women in Management Newsletter*, Women in Management Program of the National Center for Management Research and Development, Western Business School, London, Canada.

30. Ari L. Goldman, "Increasingly, Funeral Business Gets Female Touch," *New York Times*, February 15, 1992.

31. Kathleen J. Burke, conversation with author, July 1993.

32. Tamar Lewin, "Doctors Consider a Specialty Focusing on Women's Health," *New York Times*, November 7, 1992.

33. Quoted in Tiffet, "Board Gains," 38.

34. Ibid.

35. Quoted in Linda Greenhouse, "A Talk with Ginsburg on Life and the Court," *New York Times*, January 7, 1994.

36. Lotte Bailyn, *Breaking the Mold* (New York: Free Press, 1993), 11.

Chapter 8: Reforming Organizations

1. Rosabeth Moss Kanter, *Men and Women of the Corporation* (New York: Basic Books, 1977), 47.

2. Wilbert Moore, *The Conduct of the Corporation* (New York: Vintage, 1962), 109, quoted in ibid.

3. Kanter, *Men and Women of the Corporation*, 245–87.

4. Lotte Bailyn, *Breaking the Mold* (New York: Free Press, 1993), 2–3.

5. Samuel E. Bleecker, "The Virtual Organization," *Futurist*, March–April 1994.

6. Marilyn Loden and Judy Rosener, *Workforce America! Manag-*

ing Employee Diversity as a Vital Resource (Homewood, Ill.: Business One Irwin, 1991), 123–35.

7. I am indebted to Beatrice Young, president of Bea Young Associates, Inc., in Glencoe, Illinois, for this classification of stages, which was developed with her colleagues at Harbridge House Inc. and Allerton Heneghan O'Neill.

8. Jack MacAllister, "The Necessity of Diversity," *Junior League Review*, Spring 1987, 8–10.

Chapter 9: The Process of Change

1. *Stender v Lucky*, C-88-1467-MHP (DC N Calif, December 16, 1993).

2. I am indebted to Beatrice Young, president of Bea Young Associates of Glencoe, Illinois, for the concept of the change cycle.

3. This dialogue session was described to me by Beatrice Young.

4. Lee Gardenswartz and Anita Rowe, *Managing Diversity* (Homewood, Ill.: Business One Irwin, 1993), 392.

5. See also "Grooming Women for the Top," *Working Woman*, July 1994, 23–24.

6. "Deloitte Wants More Women for Top Posts in Accounting," *Wall Street Journal*, April 23, 1993.

7. For a discussion of such a methodology, see Judy B. Rosener, "User-Oriented Evaluation: A New Way to View Citizen Participation," *Journal of Allied Behavioral Science* 17, no. 4 (1981): 588–92.

8. Edward J. Chambers and Dallas M. Cullen, "Costs of Turnover among Female Managers: A Human Capital Framework," working paper series NC91-07, University of Alberta, March 1991.

9. "Equal Opportunity, Stock Performance Linked," Covenant Investment Management news release, April 21, 1993.

10. *Fortune* magazine ad, 1994.

Chapter 10: Female Underutilization Worldwide

1. Deloitte & Touche ad, *Wall Street Journal*, October 12, 1993, A12–13.

2. The European Community changed its name and became the European Union at the Maastricht Conference in 1992. Although some of the data and documents mentioned in the text predate the name change, I use the new name throughout. And while Britain is part of the European Union, I discuss it separately because it has launched some programs that are particularly instructive.

3. Readers interested in a closer analysis of the situation of women in the workplace in other countries should consult Nancy J. Adler and

Dafna N. Izraeli, eds., *Competitive Frontiers: Women Managers in a Global Economy* (Cambridge, Mass: Blackwell, 1994). See also Marilyn J. Davidson and Cary L. Cooper, eds., *European Women in Business and Management* (London: Paul Chapman, 1993).

4. Author's notes on the Equal to the Task conference, Birmingham, England, December 7, 1992.

5. "Clinton Visits University, Wins Cheers for First Lady's Role," *Los Angeles Times*, July 7, 1993.

6. *Decade of the Executive Woman*, 16; "Glass Ceiling? It's More Like a Steel Cage," *Los Angeles Times*, March 20, 1995, B8.

7. Davidson and Cooper, *European Women*, 5, 14.

8. Beverly Alimo-Metcalfe and Colleen Wedderbum-Tate, "The United Kingdom," in ibid., 16–42.

9. Commission of the European Communities, *Equal Opportunities for Women and Men*, March 1991, 7.

10. Christine Crawley, quoted in Commission of the European Communities, *Social Europe*, March 1991, 9.

11. Commission of the European Communities, "Women's Rights and Equal Opportunities," fact sheet no. 1.

12. *Social Europe*, 34.

13. My discussion of Opportunity 2000 relies heavily on Val Hammond, "Opportunity 2000: A Cultural Change Approach to Equal Opportunity," *Women in Management Review* 7, no. 7 (1992): 3–10.

14. Quoted in *Opportunity 2000 First Year Report*, October 1992.

15. Beverly Alimo-Metcalfe, "What a Waste! Women in the National Health Service," *Women in Management Review and Abstracts* 6, no. 5 (1991): 17–24.

16. Beverly Alimo-Metcalfe, "Gender and Appraisal: Findings from a National Survey of Managers in the British National Health Service," paper presented at the Global Research Conference on Women in Management, Ottawa, Canada, October 21–23, 1992.

17. Ibid.

18. "NHS Reform a Tricky Operation," *Financial Times*, December 9, 1992.

19. Quoted in Anne Stibbs, ed., *A Woman's Place* (New York: Avon Books, 1992), 217.

20. Martin Whitfield, *Independent*, November 5, 1992.

21. "Women in the NHS: An Employee's Guide to Opportunity 2000," NHS Executive Management pamphlet, September 1992.

22. Caroline Langridge, fax to author, January 8, 1995.

23. Ann James, conversation with author, June 24, 1994.

24. Langridge fax, January 8, 1995.

25. "Child-Care Leave Not Yet Firmly Established in Japan," *Japan Economic Newswire*, Kyodo News Service, March 30, 1993.

26. "Understanding Fair Employment," *Business Asia*, April 12, 1993.

27. Jennifer Cody, "To Forge Ahead, Career Women Are Venturing out of Japan," *Wall Street Journal*, August 29, 1994.

28. Nancy Adler, co-editor of *Competitive Frontiers*, conversation with author, Academy of Management meeting, August 1993.

29. Sumiko Iwao, *The Japanese Woman* (New York: Free Press, 1993), 153.

30. Adler and Izraeli, *Competitive Frontiers*, 93.

31. Quoted in Dennis Laurie, *Yankee Samurai* (New York: Harper-Business, 1992), 201.

32. Iwao, *The Japanese Woman*, 179.

33. Laurie, *Yankee Samurai*, 276. See also Iwao, *The Japanese Woman*, 63.

34. Iwao, *The Japanese Woman*, 144.

35. David E. Sanger, "The Career and the Kimono," *New York Times Magazine*, May 30, 1993.

36. I conducted this survey in cooperation with European Women's Management Development, an organization of professional women in Europe. The American women surveyed included executive women in a wide variety of professions and industries. The four-page survey questionnaire included sections on organizational data, work environment, employee utilization, and personal data. The conclusions are based on over two hundred responses. The information on Japanese women comes from the same questionnaire, distributed in a survey conducted in Japan by Mitsuyo Arimoto as part of an independent study for an M.B.A. at the University of California, Irvine. The Japanese women were also interviewed after they completed the written questionnaires.

37. Faye J. Crosby, *Relative Deprivation and Working Women* (New York: Oxford University Press, 1982).

38. Yumiko Ono, "Irked Brides in Japan Practice a New Rite: Ditching the Groom," *Wall Street Journal*, January 4, 1993.

What It All Means

1. Alexis de Tocqueville, *Democracy in America* (New York: Vintage Books, 1945), vol. 2, bk. 3, 225.

2. Phillip Harris, *High Performance Leadership*, rev. ed. (Amherst, Mass.: Human Resource Development Press, 1994), xi.

3. Quoted in Oline Luinenberg and Stephen Osborne, *The Little Pink Book* (Pulp Press, 1990), 81.

Index

RE-

Where are you on the scale (skilled—aware)

1. Show understanding (restating)
2. Finding the good
3. Listening + weighing another view
4. Staying away from 'always'
    'never'
5. Finding time + date to discuss
6. Acknowledging 'feeling'
7. Creative ways to problem solve.
8. Good body language
9. Not interrupting
10.